Early Development and Education of the Child

Early Development and Education of the Child

by Willi Hoffer

edited by Marjorie Brierley

JASON ARONSON
NEW YORK • LONDON

CLASSICAL PSYCHOANALYSIS AND ITS APPLICATIONS

A Series of Books
Edited by Robert Langs, M.D.

Contents

Foreword

Within scientific communities, it has become customary to mark significant dates in the life of a respected colleague by a volume of papers written in his honour. But, fitting as such a procedure may be, it does not compare with the tribute paid to an author by the collection and publication of his own writings, either in his life-time or "in memoriam," after his death. More than any other acknowledgment, this serves to highlight the significance of a man's work for the discipline to which he has devoted his efforts.

In this spirit, Dr. Willi Hoffer's friends, colleagues and pupils will be gratified by the appearance of this book which gives evidence not only of the bulk of his scientific preoccupations and his concern with teaching and lecturing, but also recreates a vivid picture of his personality.

Like many analysts before and after him, W. Hoffer was fascinated by what he himself called "the no man's land between biology and psychology," i.e., the slow birth of an individual's psychic personality out of the surrounding matrix of body matters, drives, needs, and emerging functions. Part I of the book before us presents to the reader his most important pronouncements on this topic. Foremost among them is the paper on "Mouth, Hand and Ego-Integration (1947)," on which many analytic authors on early development now base their further conclusions.

Unlike many others, Hoffer brought to the study of this dark area more than the powers of a speculative mind. In the absence of verbal communication with his objects of research, and faced with the uncertainties of reconstructive material, he did not hesitate to add direct observation to his armament. During the war years, he spent hours watching, scrutinizing and photographing infants in the first two years of life. His thoughts on the development of the body ego and on interaction between id and ego are derived from this source; so are his enquiries into the early stages of aggression. He studied the processes by which the pain barrier, narcissism, and the mother's libidinization of her infant's body deflect the aggressive impulse from the "internal milieu" and turn it toward the external world. He was particularly intrigued by the example of an abnormal case in which these common responses were missing—with the result that the child made ferocious, self-destructive biting attacks on her own body.

The organizers of the Hampstead War Nurseries are still proud of the fact that it was their infant departments which played such a vital role in the growth of Hoffer's scientific theories.

Part II of the book fulfills a different function for the reader. It harks back to the period before W. Hoffer was a recognized and distinguished analyst of adults, and revives the time when he was not only an enthusiastic psychoanalytic teacher of teachers, but himself passionately interested in educational experiments. As a friend and co-worker of Siegfried Bernfeld, he shared the latter's concern with adolescents and their problems, their short or prolonged spells of creativity, their fights against the recurrence of obsolete forms of sexuality or against the advent of new and age-adequate ones. There are many workers in education all over the world today who owe to Hoffer and his hitherto scattered writings their first initiation into the difficulties of thier profession.

Altogether there seems to me good hope that the forthcoming selection from Hoffer's writings will be greeted with satisfaction by a significant section of readers involved in the problems of psychoanalysis, of early development and, in general, of the young.

Anna Freud
London

Preface

Willi Hoffer wrote far more than he ever allowed to appear in print. He was very careful, sometimes perhaps overcautious, about publication. His concern has been respected in this volume. With but one exception the chapters are either reprints of papers in English or translations from the German of papers publishing during his Vienna period. The exception is chapter 7, the Freud Anniversary Lecture, delivered at the New York Psychoanalytic Institute in the spring of 1966. Since it was known that he intended to publish this, it seemed legitimate to include it.

When Willi Hoffer returned to Vienna in 1919, he at first thought of training as a veterinary surgeon. However, he soon became involved in Siegfried Bernfeld's Baumgarten Children's Home, where his interest was diverted to teaching. He subsequently met Dr. Hermann Nunberg, who as his training analyst helped him become the professional psychoanalyst that he remained for the rest of his life. Before leaving for England in 1936 he became a member of the Vienna Psychoanalytical Society, a training analyst, and a lecturer in child psychology. In spite of this change in career he never lost his interest in education. Thus, at the suggestion of Dr. Jason Aronson, these papers are arranged in two sections, reflecting these dual interests.

The author's most important contributions to psychoanalysis relate to the earliest stages of ego development (chapters 1 to 4). They stemmed from his observations (sometimes filmed) of infant feeding behavior at the Hampstead War Nurseries. He noticed that the association of mouth and hand in feeding led to the early integration of mouth and hand with libidinization of the hand, finger-sucking thus becoming a palliative for frustration; moreover, this primal integration gradually extended from mouth and hand to such other functions of the body as vision. He did not suppose that feeding behavior comprises the whole story of body-ego development, but this in no way detracts from the significance of his conclusions. He himself accepted the Harmann, Kris and Loewenstein view "put forward with the support of impressive arguments" that ego and id are differentiated from an undifferentiated state. Strictly speaking, his findings are consonant with theories other than Hartmann's, with, for example, Edward Glover's ego-nuclei hypotheses, and do not contradict the views of Winnicott and Guntrip on the crucial importance of the motehr-infant relation to "self" development.

The remaining three chapters of Part I contain a good deal of repetition, conveying to American audiences the main theses of the preceding papers. Thus Chapters 5 and 6 are two of the Abraham Flexner Lectures delivered at the Vanderbilt University Medical School, and chapter 7 is the Freud Anniversary Lecture mentioned earlier. However, all three lectures contained new material as well. For instance, chapter 5 notes how much the development of child psychiatry as a separate discipline owes to the initiative of Anna Freud and cites the implications of separation anxiety for pediatrics, psychiatry, and social organization. It summarizes the work done by Anna Freud, John Bowlby, and others on young children in hospital, which has thrown so much light on this topic. Chapter 6 describes the transition from defense to ego psychology, summarizing in addition the author's views on the earliest stages of ego development.

Chapter 7 (the Freud Anniversary Lecture) contains a further summary of early ego development but offers as well material based on his unpublished work, including a consideration of the effects of "swaddling" and a discussion of narcissism. Willi Hoffer came to regard primary narcissism as the functional aspect of primary identification. This he pushed back into deep sleep though it has more often been thought to be the primary state of consciousness (see chapter 4). It is known that this paper was to be expanded before publication, but the only hint of the author's intentions is given by jottings on scraps of paper. These include a girl's name, possibly having some connection with the next note, "demand of the drives; external demands." Whether he meant to go further into the way in which the ego succeeds or fails in reconciling these demands can only be guesswork. A query—"What is memory? 1. inborn species characteristic; 2. trauma, organization, repetition"—may have been stimulated by his reading of the symposium on psychic trauma (Basic Books, 1967). The lecture would undoubtedly have benefited had Willi Hoffer lived to carry out his intended expansion and revision.

The papers in Part II are arranged with regard to their content rather than in chronological order. The first, chapter 8, tells the story of a "Group Development in a School Community"—the Baumgarten Children's Home. This was Willi Hoffer's first publication, and the German original turned out to be a monograph unsuitable for inclusion in this volume. This chapter is therefore a much shortened version, almost a precis, of the complete work. It is hoped that the essential data have been retained but much has had to be left out, including graphs and tables. These must have cost many hours of devoted work in the effort to satisfy the statistical requirements of scientific reporting, but they add nothing to the information given in the text. The reason for the leaders quitting the Home and the resulting dissolution of the Group are not given in this story, possibly for reasons of discretion, but they are to be found in chapter 9, written many years after, in 1965.

Chapter 9, "Siegfried Bernfeld and 'Jerubaal'," was written with the help of Robert Weltsch of the Leo Baeck Institute in London. It not only gives an account of Bernfeld's journalistic and educational work but a good deal more information about the Baumgarten Children's Home. This paper is also of biographical interest since it was Bernfeld who introduced the author to Hermann Nunberg.

The next two chapters are full translations of early German papers, centering on two different types of play. Chapter 10 records a striking instance in which two boys' imaginary story about a much desired goatcart changed in character as the result of disappointment. At first the initiator of the game, Raimund, believed that his father had promised him a real goat and cart. While this gift was confidently expected, the imaginary treatment of the goat and the fantasied rides in the cart both conformed to what would have been suitable for a live goat and real cart. When Raimund was told that the goat and cart could not be obtained, the nature of the play altered entirely. The imaginary goat was removed from what would have been adequate stabling behind Raimund's home to a totally unsuitable shed in the grandmother's garden; he was milked, the milk sold, and even cheese manufactured. In short, from the imaginary play being realistic in content, it became incredibly fantastic, resentment against the father being indicated by moving the stabling from home to the grandmother's garden, the admission of the coplayer's sister to the game, and a gift of the goat's milk to the mother. The paper points out the specific features of fantasy play, that is, its reliance on imagination alone without the aid of any external paraphernalia. It also attempts to put the goat fantasy into a wider context of fantasy gratification and repression in the latency period.

Chapter 11, "The Archaic Play," illustrates, by describing a boys' "soldier" game, the way in which primitive customs can be reactivated in play. Boys wishing to join this game had to undergo an "initiation" which involved not only quasi-military training but symbolic rebirth. The author also notes that initiation ceremonies still persist in civilized life—in academic, religious and other circles in the form of examinations, and qualification—and indicates the generic components of all such rites.

Chapter 12 maintains the educational value of fairy tales and describes how they can be used to lighten the burden of repression— though child listeners must have attained a certain degree of ego development before they can profit from such holidays from duress.

Chapter 13 tells the pathetic story of a boy's struggle against masturbation, as revealed in his diary, a story that ended in mental illness from which he fortunately made a good recovery. This paper is a kind of textual analysis, using lingual clues to piece out the latent meaning of entries in the diary.

The final chapter is both an historical survey and a discussion of the actual and potential relation of psychoanalysis to education. It appeared in 1945 in the first volume of the journal *The Psychoanalytic Study of the Child.* So much has happened since then that in some respects the paper is rather out of date. Nevertheless, that Willi Hoffer's influence in this sphere is not inconsiderable is attested by the fact that the Reiss-Davis Child Study Center (Los Angeles) devoted the whole of its 1968 spring *Bulletin* to his memory. Among other appreciative contributions, this issue contained an excellent summary of the Vienna papers of Rudolf Ekstein.

Because of his warm and lively interest in people, Willi Hoffer was both a good teacher and a good clinician, perhaps most thoroughly at home in his consulting room. As Dr. William T. Orr noted while introducing him to his Vanderbilt audience, "He remains a therapist." While doubtful about some modern developments in technique, he recognized the value of reconstruction. Because of his long association with Hermann Nunberg, he was asked to give the Memorial Address for the latter in New York in 1966. This afforded a good example of his skill in coping with a difficult patient, but it cannot be published for discretionary reasons. In this address he admitted to sharing Nunberg's interest in therapy, that borderland where the theory and the practice of psychoanalysis meet. In 1936, when he arrived in London, he was understandably rather shocked by the ferment of controversy he found at work in the British Society, but this forced him to widen his horizon and to take a more active and critical interest in theory. At first this seemed a painful necessity, but he soom came to terms with it. Both he and his wife took part in the scientific discussions held from 1943 to 1945. Then and throughout his analytic career, he remained faithful to basic Freudian principles. Toward the end of his life he described himself as a "classicist," for whom Freud was a "guide" but not a "gospel."

After 1956, Hoffer's published output began to decline for one very simple reason: as his status in psychoanalysis grew, so did his lecturing and other commitments. He made numerous visits to the United States, to Israel, and particularly to continental Europe, doing a great deal to encourage the revival of psychoanalysis in postwar West Germany. As well as taking his full share in the training of candidates, in 1954 he was appointed Consultant to the Maudsley and Bethlem Hospital. He was President of the British Society from 1959 to 1962 and a most successful Editor of the *International Journal of Psycho-Analysis* from 1949 to 1959, in itself an exacting task. Public engagements were numerous, for example, a contribution on depression to a Cambridge symposium and reminiscences of the original Vienna Society, of which he was one of the few surviving members, addressed to the medical Section of the British Psychological Society. Add to this the sad loss of his wife in 1961 and the heart attack a year or two later that ushered in the decline in his own health, and it will be evident that he had scant time for the careful revision he liked to make before publication. This his services to psychoanalysis should not be measured by the amount of his published work. His unrecorded teaching and training work, his public and international relations, were major contributions in themselves. The speeches made both at his seventieth birthday banquet and at the memorial meeting held in London in October, 1968 provide ample testimony to the warmth of his personality and his benign influence.

Acknowledgments

Thanks for permission to reprint are due to the Editors of *The Psychoanalytic Study of the Child* and *The International Journal of Psycho-Analysis*; to Vanderbilt University for the Abraham Flexner Lectures and the provision of a spare copy; to the New York Psychoanalytic Institute for the Freud Anniversary Lecture and to Robert Weltsch for allowing "Siegfried Bernfeld and 'Jerubbaal'" to be reprinted from the *Leo Baeck Bulletin*.

Anna Freud's kind provision of a Foreword is much appreciated; nothing would have pleased Willi Hoffer more. I must also thank Mr. Masud Khan for much kindness and help; Dr. J. J. Sandler for useful information; and Miss Helen Boxall for supplying missing data. I am most grateful to my collaborator in translation, Vroni Gordon, who did so much hard work reading and correcting my rough drafts and making fair copies. She agreed that the Baumbarten paper was inordinately long but has no responsibility for the shortened version which appears as chapter 8.

Marjorie Brierley
Keswick, Cumbria

PART I

PSYCHOANALYSIS

AND EARLY

DEVELOPMENT

1

Mouth, Hand, and Ego Integration

What Bertram Lewin (1946) called oral psychology is a complex subject. It encompasses not only the familiar aspects of the oral drive in infancy and its vicissitudes in later life but also such remote aspects as oral eroticism and skin sensitivity (Fenichel, 1942), hypnagogic phenomena in states of fever (Isakower, 1942), the structure of delusions, and finally a detail in the psychology of dreams, called the dream screen.

While acknowledging that the work of psychoanalysts is not lacking in hard research and ingenious imagination, one still wonders whether its tentative and experimental character is sufficiently recognized and whether generalization will come about before the comparative slowness of analytic practice has permitted the full re-examination and final assessment of innovations.

In his admirable study, "Sleep, the Mouth and the Dream Screen," Bertram Lewin (1946) puts forward the view that in the sleeper's mind the psychic residue (unconscious memory) of his mother's breast is represented as a dream screen on which the dreamer projects his dreams. He also thinks that when falling asleep and regressing to an objectless, fetal state, we pass through an early oral stage of mental organization. On this process he throws a powerful light.

The difficulties that psychoanalysts face when discussing mental processes in early infancy are caused by the absence of the familiar functions of an ego and superego which reveal, through speech and other external indications, the psychic reality underlying human activities. The instincts themselves cannot be studied directly: they "are superb in their indefiniteness," and "we are never certain that we are seeing them clearly" (Freud, 1933).

Much, if not everything, therefore depends on the detection of those early functions which either germinate from an inborn ego core (Jeanne Lampl-de Groot, 1947) or present themselves as the first results of differentiation from the id. They belong to the no-man's-land between biology and psychology which Freud called "Biological Psychology." From the exploration of these early stages of mental life we have to learn that the ego, as a contour, is inherited and its differentiation from the id phylogenetically outlined.

In the following investigation I shall enlarge on the idea that the differentiation of the ego from the id (Hartmann, Kris, Loewenstein, 1946) shows itself on the infant's body-surface when, in the service of the oral partial instinct and for the sake of autoerotic pleasure, two sensations—one oral and one tactile—are aroused simultaneously by finger-sucking. Such a situation does not usually arise before the twelfth week when, intentionally and no longer reflexively, the hand is put into the mouth in order to relieve oral tension.

In general psychology the function of the hand has mainly been studied as that of an organ which grasps. I am not suggesting that before this grasping function manifests itself, the hand is merely an attachment to the mouth, but that from intrauterine life onward it becomes closely *allied* to the mouth for the sake of relieving tension and, within this alliance, leads to the first achievement of the primitive ego. From that point on the hand cannot relinquish the function of relieving tension, and in this way it becomes the most useful and versatile servant of the ego.

Having in mind these far-reaching implications of infantile finger-sucking, I now propose to follow a systematic line of presentation.

The observations to which I shall refer are taken partly from the writings of Gesell and Ilg (mainly from their book on the feeding behavior of infants, 1937) and partly from observations which I was privileged to make at the Hampstead (War) Nurseries with the active support of Anna Freud and Dorothy Burlingham and their co-workers (Burlingham and Freud, 1943, Anna Freud, 1946 and 1947).

According to Gesell the hand-to-mouth response is anticipated *in utero.* Many years ago, Preyer (1895), stated that the fetus introduces its fingers into its mouth and thus elicits the first sensation of touch on its own body.

How does the hand of the fetus or newborn child reach the mouth? In intrauterine life the fist is brought into contact with the sensitive oral zone because the posture of the fetus adjusts itself to the concavity of the uterus in such a way that the hand or fist is nearest to the chin or mouth. Touching the face elicits the sucking reflex in the fetus and newborn infant. Up to the second quarter of the first year, sucking depends entirely on touch though afterward it will also be initiated by the sight of the breast or bottle (Gesell and Ilg, 1937).

Does the infant show any preference for the breast or bottle in contrast to the hand during the first twelve weeks? This question must be answered in the negative. At first neither breast, bottle nor hand, but only the touching of the oral zone elicits sucking movements. Gesell states that sometimes it is necessary to hold the hands down to prevent the fingers and the nipple from being sucked together. From about the twelfth week onward the infant shows progressively greater differentiation between breast (bottle) and hand. The hand serves the need for oral pleasure (sucking) only, whereas breast and bottle serve both the need for sucking and for food. From the twelfth week onward, the hand helps in the sucking process by being placed half open on the breast or bottle. From 16 weeks on a more definite grasping response may occur when the infant, on seeing the bottle, grasps it as it is brought to his mouth. During feeding his hands are placed more firmly around the bottle or on the breast.

Turning now to the infants in the Hampstead Nurseries, the most striking fact in their sucking behavior was the directness and resolution with which, from the twelfth week on, the infants made their fingers approach and enter their mouths. This could be observed at any time during waking hours but was of course accentuated before and immediately after feeding. The hand may be introduced by the shortest route or by a wide circle of the arm while the eyes may follow the movements of the hand. In infants of that age I could seldom observe vigorous sucking movements when the fingers entered the mouth, in contrast to the response when the bottle was brought to the mouth. Finger-sucking is mainly a rhythmic, intensive, and pleasurable sucking. Its duration seems to be more important than its intensity. It may stop for a shorter or longer period while the hand hangs on the mandible with fingers bent, indicating irritation of the gums due to teething.

Bertie, a boy of 16 weeks, is an experienced finger-sucker who suspends his ring finger in his mouth by bending the three remaining fingers and pressing them like a scaffolding toward his lower lip, thsu preventing his hand from sliding into his mouth. One cannot overlook the high degree of adaptation the infant achieves in easing oral tension. The hand skillfully adapts itself to the needs of the oral zone; its shape and volume are changed from fist to one small finger according to the need for stimulation. Finger or fist can penetrate deeply or slightly into the mouth and can be directed toward its inner or outer structures. The versatility of the hand in the sucking process allows for originality and elaboration of individual pleasure patterns in great numbers. Regarding Bertie's "scaffolding," I have one observation to make: Bertie was breastfed for the first seven weeks while he was still at home. It may be that a tactile sensation was aroused on his chin or lower lip by his mother's hand holding the nipple in his mouth. The position of his fingers while finger-sucking might therefore also be interpreted as a voluntary reproduction of an epidermal stimulation which he felt when sucking at the breast.

Another example of a genuine and self-directed hand to mouth movement was observed in Tom, when 16 weeks old. He had never been breastfed but had been brought up on the bottle in a most satisfactory way. Filmed sucking his thumb, he revealed unusual effort and exertion for a 16-week-old child. He held his arms slightly bent in front of his face; the fingers were stretched, and those of the left hand tried to grasp the right thumb with a pincer movement. While both hands tried to get closer to each other with jerky movements, Tom's mouth was kept open, he made an effort as if he were trying to lift his head, and his lips sucked in air like a turbine. When he succeeded in catching his thumb and introducing it into his mouth, his left hand was then held over his mouth, locking it and preventing his right hand from sliding out again. If it did slide out, his left hand quickly pushed it back again and his thumb was pushed far back toward the palate, accompanied by quite intensive sucking. No other form of oral greed in connection with food was observed in Tom.

In the case of Bertie we said that his hand achieved a high degree of adaptation for sucking, for increasing and probably varying the autoerotic pleasure. In Tom's case both hands (and arms) operate together. One hand, though with the greatest difficulty, grasps the other, as some weeks later it grasps inanimate objects.

Gesell and Ilg (1942) say of the 16-week-old baby that he brings his fingers together over his chest and engages them in mutual fingering play. His fingers finger his fingers! Thus he himself touches and is being touched simultaneously. This double touch is a lesson in self-discovery. He comes to appreciate what his fingers are and that objects are something different. In Gesell's view the eyes lead and the hands follow. This principle applies to a baby learning to control the outer world; it does not apply to the baby learning to know its own body: he learns it by touching one hand with the other and by touching his mouth.

The association of hand and mouth may become so close that it can interfere temporarily with the feeding process and the feeding function of the mouth. The infant may insist either on sucking his fingers at the same time that he is being fed, or may refuse to be fed at all because of his wish to suck his fingers only. While Gesell records this observation as if it were an accidental interference with the feeding process caused by the hand, our Hampstead Nurseries film leads us to interpret this behavior as competition between the feeding process and finger-sucking.

The necessity of holding the hands down to prevent fingers and breast (or bottle or spoon) being sucked at the same time, as Gesell states, has probably obscured this competitive behavior on the part of the infant. Winnicott (1945), however, mentions that "some babies put a finger in the mouth while sucking the breast, thus (in a way) holding on to self-created reality while using external reality." This behavior could be observed quite frequently in infants from about the fourteenth week onward. In one case the infant adds his thumb to the bottle in the mouth and insists on its remaining there while he is fed; in another case he tolerates the bottle well without interfering by finger-sucking, but starts to introduce the finger immediately when fed spinach with a spoon.

In looking for an explanation of this behavior, we cannot prove that competition with the fingers aims at *prevention* of feeding. The bottle or spoon was not rejected in all casses in which the finger was added. This can mean that the child while being fed did not experience the expected or accustomed oral stimulation in the feeding act itself and therefore reverted to the accustomed autoerotic stimulation of the oral zone by finger-sucking. This shows the infant's preference for the repetition of known and experienced gratification. The negative reaction to abrupt changes of stimulus and the importance of acquired habits of keeping sensory stimulation within certain limits, high or low as the case may be, has perhaps not been taken into account sufficiently in child psychology. The troublesome fussing of the infant when put to the breast, described by Gesell and Ilg (1937) and Middlemore (1941), may justifiably be viewed as the infant's dislike of a too abrupt change from a low to a high level of stimulation or the reverse.

The competition may persevere for some weeks. The range of activities widens rapdily during the second and third quarters of the first year, and no longer reflects an exclusive preference for the oral zone. I am inclined to believe that the hands, after being libidinized during the intensive sucking period, now function more independently of the oral zone and are more under the influence of the eyes, playing the part of an intermediary between eyes and mouth. They have developed from instruments serving as a means for discharging tension into tools which control the outer world. At this stage they have become a most active extension of the growing ego.

In studying early ego functions, we have to take into account that the customary feeding methods very early deny the infant the pleasureable use of his hands when he is being fed. The newborn child needs to be fed actively, the breast or bottle has to enter the mouth, and the hand is still unable to help or to participate in the feeding process. It does not provide food, it provides oral pleasure. The more breast and bottle are superseded by semisolid and solid food, the more important do mug, spoon, and hand become as instruments. Instead of the accustomed soft nipple, which remains in the mouth, the hard spoon or mug touches or enters it—with increasing frequency—leaving it after a very short time to be refilled and put back again. The accustomed feeding method consists in feeding by the bottle, mug, and spoon until the baby has gained full control of his movements so that he can feed himself, which usually starts during the second year. Modern feeding methods, as practiced in the Hampstead Nurseries, allow the child to feed himself before the end of the first year. The transition is a gradual one, from spoon-feeding out of a bowl by the adult to the next stage, when the infant grasps the spoon and follows its movement to the mouth. It often happens, of couse, that the infant puts his hands into the bowl and splashes the food but, as soon as he develops enough skill, he directs his hands from bowl to mouth, and thus feeding entirely by his own hands has begun. This leads eventually to self-feeding by spoon. This self-feeding training coincides with the oral-sadistic stage, the stage of teething and biting.

Surprisingly enough it very rarely happens that a child bites his own hand, though he may quite often fail to keep balance and may drop the food just as the fingers have been put into the mouth. Contrary to expectation the infant shows a high regard for his hands and will not go further than chewing his fingers occasionally.

.

Although bodily injury is very frequent at this stage—if the child is given a fair opportunity to move about—the teeth are very rarely the cause of self-injury, although licking and biting are practiced on toys and on the crib. We might say that the child who likes himself will not bite himself. It is the first triumph of primitive narcissism over a parital instinct like the oral-sadistic instinct, and the child achieves this victory without being protected by his mother. This principle does not apply in the same degree to the infant's food at this age, since there may be some oral-sadistic handling of the food. Nevertheless, in general, the infant treats his food and his hands with care and regard, at any rate for some months, until the anal-sadistic stage has been fully reached. In the control of oral-sadism toward solid food, paradoxical as it may sound, the infant has taken his first step toward the acquisition of eating manners by imposing on himself the first restrictions in handling food, for instance by biting it slowly and into tiny bits. Semisolid food is devoured, the hand being used merely as a shovel.

Simultaneously with the appearance of the teeth and of biting, the arms and hands develop far beyond the original hand-mouth relationship. We have said that at first hand and mouth convey the primal sensation of self. Then the hand associates itself with the eyes and other sense-organs, particularly with the sense of equilibrium, in which the infant's arms and hands are of great importance. During the short quadrupedal phase of motor development the child's hands are more frequently in contact with the ground than ever before or after. The innate urge to put the hands up to the face consequently leads to stimulation of the olfactory system as well.

Considering too the fact that the infant puts everything that is within reach into his mouth with the help of his hands, by the end of the first year the accumulation of experience as a result of the mouth and hand relationship seems to be rich and promising. We can therefore safely assume that, on entering his second year, the infant has built up an oral-tactile concept of his own body and by this means regulates to a certain extent his erotic and aggressive (active) drives.

2

Oral Aggressiveness and Ego Development

The assumption that little progress in our knowledge of infantile life can be expected from mere observation can easily be proved erroneous. Psychoanalytic hypotheses which have not yet been put to the test can still be used as starting-points for further observation and resesarch, and chance experiments which nature itself provides from time to time have proved fruitful. Guided by the psychoanalytic method, we shall see more in infants and children and know more about them if only we make the attempt to do so.

Thus, on the basis of infantile finger-sucking, I have suggested that the mouth-hand relationship enables us to visualize the route by which the growing ego travels when developing from the primitive mouth-ego to the more mature body-ego. This line of study may also make accessible to direct observation the process by which the ego and the id become differentiated (Hoffer, 1949).

In the present investigation, a similar approach will be taken to another problem of contemporary psychoanalysis. Once again, by using observations of oral behavior, some light may be thrown on the relation of oral aggressiveness and destructiveness in early ego development. These observations were made under the favorable conditions existing in the Hampstead (War) Nurseries, with the encouragement and support of their Directors, Dorothy Burlingham and Anna Freud (cf Dorothy Burlingham and Anna Freud, 1943). I also wish to express my thanks for the valuable help I received when making and checking these observations from Miss Sophie Dann, Sister-in-Charge of the Babies Department and Miss Gertrude Dann, who was in charge of the Department for "Junior Toddlers."

OBSERVATION

In December, 1941, an infant girl, three-and-one-half months old, was admitted, together with her mother, to the residential Hampstead (War) Nurseries and stayed there—with one interruption of nine months duration—until the age of three-and-one-half years. She was the illegitimate child of a manic-depressive mother and an unknown soldier. She was breastfed on entering the Nurseries and until she was ten months old. For some periods an attempt was made to substitute a bottle for the breast, sometimes with success. The child's weight at birth 5½ lbs., doubling after four months, and trebling after eight months. On admission the baby vomited frequently and the time of taking her at the breast had to be shortened to ten minutes for each feeding, when the vomiting stopped; she put on weight and lost it for no obvious reason.

After some weeks of observation signs of physical and mental retardation became more and more apparent. While the development of bodily functioning was steady though very slow, both bodily skill and social responses were subject to sudden changes and variations. For some periods the girl remained unaffected by the mother's changes of mood; on other occasions she responded very quickly by screaming. When at the age of six months, the infant was offered a bottle by the mother, she turned her head away and refused to take it; subsequently she started to bite her own hands and later bit herself most violently and with visible effect. When the baby was nine months, the mother worried about whether or not she should start weaning; the baby had bit the breast, refused it, and smacked it with her fists. She then took food well from a spoon; at times she refused it altogether and took only liquids. Screaming and spitting were the signs of refusal. Later, after her first birthday, her slowness of movement spread to the feeding process itself, and for long periods she seemed to fall asleep while being fed.

From eleven months on, the infant's reactions to her mother's changing moods became definite. Often, when the mother was in an excited state, the child reacted by screaming. At the age of one year and two months, she started to rock and to stare at a fixed point; this was very characteristic of her later behavior.

At the age of one year and seven months the child underwent a severe crisis. She had just succeeded in saying "Mummy" (in addition to her only other word, "No") when her mother's condition deteriorated to such an extent that confinement in a mental hospital was necessary. This meant separation from her daughter for about two months. Earlier, the little girl had displayed head banging, which became worse at night. Sometimes the banging was accompanied by pleasure and smiles, sometimes by screaming, sometimes it was done in silence.

Shortly after the mother's return from the mental hospital, the girl contracted ringworm (at one year ten months). She had lately shown some signs of progressive development and had started to play with other children and to chew her fingers instead of sucking them The child was moved into a hospital for special treatment—an unhappy period of nine months, including a period of quarantine for scarlet fever.

After her return from hospital (at the age of two years and seven moths) she refused solid food from others and did not take it herself when left alone. For periods she had to be fed by force. She bit her hands and arms, which had to be kept bandaged to protect them. She cried incessantly for long periods and knocked her head quite forcefully against the wall but two months later she did not need bandages and would eat everything. Some time later she again began to bite herself still more violently without any traceable cause. There was a short period in which she liked to pinch her mother and other adults who entered the room, but eventually social withdrawal became the rule, with everyone, even her mother. She refused food, lost weight, and finally was accepted in a hospital for mental defectives under the M.D. Act. There her development took a quite favorable course—within the limits of mental defectiveness. She has ceased to bite herself except occasionally, when her mother visits her.

Observations like these corroborate the claim that strong and vehement aggressive strivings operate in and must be dealt with by the child during its early years. But while the intensity and forcefulness of the oral aggressive components of the instinctual drives is fully recognized, we enter the realm of controversy when we come to discuss the possible aim and object of the self-biting and its developmental significance. According to current psychoanalytic theory, self-destructiveness, or aggression turned against one's own body in early childhood, has one of three possible causes: one possible focus is the child's overwhelmingly *strong, self-destructive drive* which interferes with normal development. Significantly, in the case of this girl, turning her head away from the mother and biting herself did not occur before the second half of the first year, which is the period of preoccupation with teething and the stage of oral sadism. Why, we ask, was this urge to bite, to cause pain, perhaps to destroy, turned against the child's own body and not against the mother?

This leads us to the second hypothesis—the *"primal object love"* postulated by Ferenczi's school, especially by Alice Balint (1939) and Michael Balint (1937). These workers maintain that there exists from birth onward a "Dual Unity," a genuine object relationship, not merely between mother and child (that is self-evident), but between mother and neonate as well. Breach of the "Dual Unity" evokes dramatic reactions which may become paramount in later life. The argument in this case might therefore be that the manic-depressive mother was subject to alternations of mood which were noticed by the infant, so that it turned its head away. Subsequently, the infant had given up not only the object of its love but also of its hate, which it then turned against its own body.

This explanation leaves a wide gap between the phenomena observed and those which might justly be expected when there is an interruption of an object relationship in early childhood. There were no transitory reactions, no warning signs: the infant did not show unpleasure about the mother, did not cry for her or display other signs of disappointment. The only distinct sign of disturbance of the girl's object relationship was the opposite to a longing for a satisfactory object—i.e., the need for avoiding contact with the mother as an object.

Perhaps we have to think much more deeply, in terms of *inner conflicts and of inner forces* opposing each other and struggling for hegemony within ourselves. Three sources of inner conflict are known. A conflict can exist (a) between instinctual drives (but such "biologic" conflict in the infant, though we can conceive it in our imagination, is difficult to substantiate at such an early age); or (b) within the ego, which is then subjected to an onslaught of instinctual demands tending towards conflicting goals; or (c) a so-called "structual conflict," i.e., one involving the three strata of the differentiated psyche. Childhood, adolescence, the psychoses and, above all, our daily experience give testimony to the existence and acuteness of such inner conflicts. But some degree of differentiation of psychic structure—to follow Hartmann, Kris and Loewenstein (1946)—must have taken place if we are to conceive of conflicting interests operating in the mind. Accordingly some psychoanalysts such as Melanie Klein (1945) will assume that what the girl displayed in her self-destructive biting was a superego conflict, others will assume various mechanisms of a differentiated ego (e.g., ambivalence), while still others will question the appropriateness of the term "inner conflict" in such a case. On one point, however, we can expect agreement, namely, on the enormous complexity of mental functioning in the first year of life and its close connection with bodily functions.

The general pathology of mental defectiveness does not concern us here, but in so far as self-destructiveness does, we shall learn more if we turn our attention to the more normal phenomena of infancy. The question waiting to be answered is not only why does a defective child bite itself but also why do infants passing through a most active stage of oral organization, and especially through that called oral sadism, *not* usually bite themselves?

CONCEPT OF ORAL AGGRESSIVENESS

To what extent do we assume that infantile aggressiveness can operate in the infant? To give the widest possible answer, I propose to use the term "aggressiveness"—meaning the result of outward deflection of aggression—in its broadest sense and to include under the definition any form of muscular activity, real or imagined, so long as this usage makes sense and helps us to solve our problem.

The infant's aggressiveness can conveniently be divided into "oral" and "nonoral" and the latter can be dealt with briefly. Nonoral activities in early infancy frequently accompany oral activities and are subordinated to them; I believe them most likely to be the result of spread of excitation; the path of the spread of excitation is not chosen at random by the exciting force but is concordant with the functional necessities of the body or its parts.

Oral aggressiveness in early infancy can be ascribed to three oral-organ systems, which I enumerate according to the time at which they come into operation: (1) the mouth, which sucks and swallws even *in utero,* (2) the mouth-digestive tract, which not only takes in but eliminates orally by vomiting (throwing-up) and later by spitting, (3) the mouth respiratory tract.

In extra-uterine life the mouth learns to hold the nipple, to suck it* and, sooner or later, to manipulate it with the jaws. This last activity, the result of libidinal and aggressive strivings, has been viewed indiscriminately as if it were a *destructive biting activity.* I doubt the accuracy of this description. We should try to differentiate among three functions: first, an aggressive use of the jaws, by which is meant biting the breast, chewing it, cracking the nipple by actively working on it; second, a merely active grasping and holding of the nipple which is arrested between the jaws and actively prevented from being withdrawn so that the feeling of contact with the breast will not be interrupted; third, a hostile snapping or closing of the jaws. This last is observed in certain babies who in this way resist being forced to suck the breast, usually because they prefer the more easily flowing bottle. Some do not wish to be irritated by a hand pressing the head against the breast or by the nervousness of the mother which interferes with the intensive act of a satisfactory feed.

I believe that grasping the nipple with the lips, sucking the breasts, and using the jaws to hold on to the breast represent three degrees of contact.

This active grasping and holding the breast can, like every activity, be subject to frustration. Frustration will have one of two effects: either the activity will cease altogether, or, more frequently, the active striving will be heightened and raised to an attack. Aggressive attack as a consequence of frustration of mouth activity can be thought of as developmental progress in the possible modes of discharging tension. An earlier stage may have witnessed an outbreak of rage or a convulsive attack in which no aim-directed activity is displayed. Some years ago W. Clifford Scott (1946) reported two examples of changes in aggression to an external object when ambivalence to this object had developed. The previous aggression was replaced by a state of tension or tonus followed by a convulsive or clonic state.

Yet no *primary destructive aim* need be supposed to underlie the very young infant's *activity* itself or its mental representation, and therefore no need should arise for the child to turn aggression against its own body or self. Where this appears really to happen and not merely to be inferred by the anxious mother—as has been described in Russian mothers by Ruth Benedict and Geoffrey Gorer—a frustrating situation must have interfered with the active discharge.

Nevertheless, psychoanalytic observations during and after the teething period have proved the existence of a true oral-aggressive and sadistic stage of instinctual development. The initial instruments for its discharge are the teeth. But all the structures in the mouth may participate and function as executors of oral-sadistic strivings. There can be no doubt about the aggressive, destructive character and aim of the infant's oral attack on the mother's breast or its substitute. But in the oral-sadistic stage the breast has already become an object; it is not "me" for the baby any more. With this differentiation of an object in the outer world, a world of "me" and "not-me" has appeared in the infant's primitive mind.

LIMITATIONS OF ORAL AGGRESSIVENESS

An important negative feature of the infant's behavior must now attract our attention. Infants in the oral-aggressive stage rarely bite themselves—even if their oral sadism should be severely frustrated. From this stage on some kind of self-regard must be taken into consideration and, so long as it is operative, we should not expect the infant to turn its aggresiveness as such, uncontrolled and unmodified, against itself and its body. I shall not deal here with the infant's scratching itself or with similar activities towards its body which, in spite of their intensity, *respect the pain barrier.*

When using the term "self-regard" in relation to an infant of about three to four months onward we mean a psychological stage in which primary narcissism has already been modified but the world of objects has not necessarily yet taken on definite shape. The boundaries of a supposed self, to follow Paul Federn, are still on the move toward the body and its surface and by no means defined.

What psychological process can we conceive as being involved in this movement of cathexes towards the infant's own body?

PAIN BARRIER

It was Freud who suggested that the infant perceives pleasurable, good things as part of itself and unpleasant, bad things as not included in the self, not existing in the self. The differentiation occurs in consequence of signals received through the sensory system, mainly through the mouth, which is the first and foremost sense organ to function. But we must also think of another differentiating system in our body, that which registers the difference between "pain" and "not pain." The infant learns when communicating with the world at large (which need not at that stage be a world separated from its own self) that it has to regard the pain barrier. This barrier plays its paramount role only after free movement sets in but, from early infancy onward, it is a very potent safe-guard against the aggressive instinct's turning against the infant's own body. When *reality testing* is learned the pain barrier plays its part. If the pain barrier is disregarded, traumatic experiences occurs, followed by anxiety and inhibition of function, by withdrawal or arrest of discharge, by accumulation of aggression, by rage or attack—but hardly by self-destructiveness. The pain barrier will oppose it. (Addendum, 1950: After a recent discussion with Dorothy Burlingham I feel no hesitation in saying that, on closer inspection, the pain barrier as a psychological phenomenon appears as a broad borderland in which the distinction between pain and not-pain may become very difficult. Pain, like any other sensation, is subject within limits to ego-integration; its relation to anxiety has been definitely established by Freud.)

LIBIDINIZATION OF THE BODY

The pain barrier against self-destructiveness is reinforced by a progressive libidinization of the body. The "*mouth-self*" is extended to the "*body-self*" beginning at about the twelfth week of life. (I have discussed its libidinal aspect on the occasion of the Amsterdam Conference of European Psychoanalysts [Hoffer, 1949; chapter 1 this volume]).

The activity of the hand carries the process of libidinization from the mouth to the parts within reach and thus reinforces the stimulation exerted by the mother's care of the body.

Perhaps we may say that the hand enlarges the "mouth-self" to a "body-self" and thus helps the infant to replace the missing breast by its own warm, soft body, which, with increasing intensity, conveys the orally rooted sensation of self. We now understand why in order to maintain this achievement the normally disposed infant has hardly any motive for turning its aggression against its own body and self: it is because the infant loves itself so much.

To repeat: in deflecting the destructive instinct from the baby's own body and self, the *pain barrier* is in operation from birth. It becomes reinforced from the third month onward by the gradual development of a *self* which regulates and spreads instinctual tensions, aggressive and erotic alike.

This double protection against self-destructiveness explains the intensity of aggressiveness turned against the outer world and the subsequent increase of narcissistic feelings if this form of mastery is successful. Infantile narcissism is a protection against self-destructiveness, though not against dangers from outside or accidents. It is well known that the infant's attraction for his mother is partly due to his heightened narcissism, with which the mother likes to identify herself. In the mental economy of the infant this means receiving still more love, and this object-love can easily be conceived as a third protective barrier (in addition to the pain barrier and self-love) against the directing of aggression toward the self and the body.

Only the small child is supposed to enjoy this triple protection. In a mature, postambivalent object relationship this form of heightened narcissism ascribed to the infant is rare, and the two are perhaps incompatible. Narcissism beyond an optimum degree is a hindrance to genuine object-love and, though one may desire such love, this desire does not always find fulfilment. Its place is supplied by an increase of self-love instead of love of the object.

In old age this too fades away and one has to resort to the oldest barrier against self-destructiveness, the functioning of pain sensations. As in infancy, sure reliance can be placed on the pain barrier until it itself becomes undermined by physical or psychological patholgoy leading to the destruction of the body, the system for and in which the pain barrier functions.

3

Development of the Body Ego

Recent consideration of the genesis of mental structure has led Hartmann, Kris, and Loewenstein (1946) to advocate a modification of Freud's view of the origin of the ego as expounded by him in *The Ego and the Id* (1923). With the support of impressive arguments, they suggest that the ego should no longer be considered the result of differentiation from the id but that both the ego and the id should be conceived as joint end products of differentiation from an undifferentiated state.

Hartmann, Kris, and Loewenstein (1946) explicitly "refrained from indicating at what point in early infancy the successive steps leading to structural differentiation take place," but they state that the first and most fundamental step "concerns the ability of the infant to distinguish between the self and the world around him." This idea agrees with Freud's own thoughts on ego formation, according to which "the ego is the part of the id which has been modified by the direct influence of the external word acting through the PCS (Perpetual Conscious System).

But there is, according to Freud, another differentiating agency which, instead of being tuned to stimulation from outside, responds to stimuli from within the organ system. Under certain conditions, instinctual drives not only act on the bodily and mental apparatus but, merely by operating within the organism cause changing states of tension or demands and relaxations which are registered within the body in respect to their intensity and perhaps the locality in which they arise. I refer to the very first sensations and the earliest processes of discharge following an excitation. Freud spoke of *internal perceptions* which, in contrast to external ones, are more fundamental and more elementary.

SELF, BODY, AND OBJECT

The visual, auditory, and olfactory apparatus has a definite relation to our interest in the outer world which, in the most primitve language, is the "not-self." On this relation the environmentalists among us concentrate when studying early ego functions. In contrast, inner perception, according to Freud, seems to be related at first to the pleasure-pain series. In other words: the experience of pleasure and of a self emerges in consequence of the relief of pain (relief of stimulation calling for restoration of the previous condition or of the relief of an increase of inner demands). This relief occurs in two stages: (1) by an attempted relief due to an inner-psychical act called "negative hallucination", (2) by a physical act of discharge which we can only interpret, in the first instance, as the organism's attempt to rid itself of surplus stimulation (or inner demand).

Negative hallucination refers to the temporary hallucinatory abolition of a stimulus, inside or outside the body, one of the earliest and most primitive of mental processes, it is therefore related, in later life, to the pathological state of derealization (*Entfremdungsgefuehl*) one of the earliest and most primitive of mental processes.

Although our understanding of negative hallucination is fragmentary, we feel on firm ground as soon as we think of mental processes which characterize the spread of the feeling of self over the infant's body, in which the self is housed. When the infant's sight has been sufficiently developed so it can see its own body, the body is perceived like any other object reaching the infant's mind through the organ of vision. Quite different is the effect of the perceptual experience when the infant touches his body. Here two sensations— touching and being touched—simultaneously yield an experience. This may occur very early in life, perhaps even in the intrauterine state. Our own experience when touching the body makes us think of one part of our body, for instance the hand, actively approaching another part which passively experiences being touched. There seems no simple justification for assuming that the same happens in early infancy. Coming in touch with its own body elicits two sensations of equal quality, and these lead to the distinction between the self and the not-self, between body and what subsequently becomes environment. In consequence, this factor contributes to the processes of structural differentiation. Delimitation between the self-body and the outer world, the world where objects are found, is thus initiated.

THE MOUTH-EGO

In psychoanalysis we define the structural entity "ego" according to its functions. In our clinical work they manifest themselves in highly organized and differentiated psychic activities. In childhood and especially in infancy, these ego functions have a definite physical, bodily connotation.

In another paper (Hoffer 1949) I have described the difference between a drive (instinct) gratification as such and one interfered with by a functioning ego. To summarize it once more: there is a striking difference between infants aged up to ten weeks and those of twelve to sixteen weeks. An infant of four weeks, when slightly hungry and waiting to be fed, may display some oral activities accompanied by movements of the head, arms, and hands. The hands may still be kept in a position resembling the intrauterine, in which the hands were nearest to the mouth (Preyer, [1895]; Gesell, [1937]). While the hand is moving over the face, the mouth may get hold of it and finger-sucking will ensue. Until the infant is a few weeks old, it will not make much difference whether the whole hand or one or two fingers slip into the mouth or whether a bottle or a comforter has been offered to the baby. The behavior it displays is (a) motor excitation, probably arising from hunger and influenced by former feeding experiences (searching for the breast) and (b) numerous attempts to relieve the excitation by mouth activities which may lead to finger-sucking.

The behavior observed in a sixteen-week-old infant is quite different. Little is left to chance gratification. During the state of expectancy before being fed or after a successful feed the infant may insist on a definite form of oral sucking gratification, and the activities leading to this comply with almost all the criteria by which we assess ego functioning.

There is:

(1) Genuine *Perceptual Activity*. The infant of three months sees his hand, focuses on it, follows its movement towards the mouth with his eyes. If the infant's eyes catch another visual stimulus, especially something moving, they may be distracted but will return to the hand which tends towards the mouth. In the setting described there is true perception.

(2) *Motor Control*. The movement of the hand toward the mouth may be achieved only with great difficulty. Chance movements either are impossible or the infant counteracts them; it tries to aid the hand which is to be sucked. When the eyes participate in the control of movement toward the mouth there seems to be a pleasant realization of the space which is within reach of the arms and hands. The mouth-ego has widened to the space embraced by the arms.

(3) *Functioning of Memory*. This is suggested by the specific mode of gratification which is achieved by finger-sucking. Out of a vast free choice of possible positions of the hand and fingers, the infant develops and adheres to a number of sucking patterns, involving either his hand and fingers or his mouth or both.

(4) *Reality Testing*. We can trace the infant's reality testing by his meticulous choice of what he wishes to introduce into his mouth. When he wishes to use his fingers, he will reject the spoon or comforter or breast. Some infants display a minor feeding difficulty,

seldom mentioned, by insisting on sucking the fingers while being fed. This competition between feeding and finger-sucking seems to be a further proof of the infant's knowledge and understanding of mouth and hand in their relation to each other. No such specificity has generally been assumed for the infant's relationship to the nursing mother, the breast or the bottle, and no definite individual picture of an "object" seems as yet to have been created in the child's mind at that age. It should be possible, however, to put these problems to the test by experimentally investigating the infant's reality testing with regard to objects which do not convey the feeling of self.

(5) *Synthetic Function of the Ego.* No definite suggestion can be put forward about the operation of the synthetic function in early infancy characterizing what I call the "mouth-ego." This ignorance on our part may be due to lack of observational evidence or to the nursing mother's activity, which may make this function un- necessary at this early stage.

MOUTH-EGO AND BODY-EGO

With the help of the hand the oral sucking drive undergoes a transformation from an instinctual demand to an ego-controlled activity. In the course of this process the hand, like the mouth, is perceived as part of the self, and the differentiation between self and not-self is thus carried forward. All these processes have so far been confined to the oral phase of instinct and ego development. Sometimes the administration of breast or bottle may stimulate object relating at the expense of body-ego formation.

With the emergence of a real mouth-ego, the hand acquires the properties of a tool for the execution of needs serving the interests of the self. For example, in the first weeks of life a successful feed will be followed, almost immediately, by sleep; when the mouth-ego is established, satiation will be followed by two needs, sucking and sleep; the infant will actively introduce his fingers into his mouth and will concentrate on this activity until it is achieved. Thus finger-sucking serves the need for sleep as well. There is, we assume, no struggle between the two needs: the gratification of one leads to the gratification of the other. In this way the self has gained control of needs and achieved a form of independence, and an ability to channel instinctual drives according to earlier experiences.

In consequence, by the time the infant reaches the oral-sadistic phase, its aggressive impulses have already been drawn away from the body and directed, I assume, into oral-biting activities which do not affect the self. In short, the self seeks protection against its own aggressive feelings—originating in instinctual demands—by directing them through the body organs toward the non-self, the outer world. This involves progressive libidinization of the body and prepares the way for the integration of the subsequent instinctual stages into the ego-organization. I believe there is continuity of ego development and integrative endeavor at work, in part very successfully.

FATE OF AGGRESSION DURING THE DEVELOPMENT OF THE BODY-EGO

Progressive libidinization of the infantile body and growth of the body-ego can only be assumed if self-destructive drives are either dealt with within the body or diverted outside it. The fact that there is an increase of motor activity from the second half of the first year onward supports the second alternative. It is primarily the pain barrier which protects the infant against his destructive instincts turning against his own self (Hoffer, 1950a). In addition, owing not only to the nursing activities but also to the mouth-hand relationship, the libidinization of the body rises to the level of self-love. Increase of primary narcissism then forms a second protective barrier which develops in the oral-sadistic stage, characterized by the appearance of the teeth and heightened oral-aggressive stimulation. The infant does not hurt himself because he likes himself so much. This statement does not contradict the concept of erotogenic masochism but, when speaking here of self-destructiveness, I intend that it should be understood literally. When steps towards deflection of self-destructiveness fail, damage to the self by biting, refusal of food, and starvation open up the subject of the pathology of the body-ego.

CLINICAL IMPLICATIONS OF THE BODY-EGO

From what has been said of the path of early ego development it seems to me conceivable that, except for the experience of birth, the infant is equipped with the means of achieving equilibrium among his inner needs without necessarily being traumatized. Still, infants may have to pass through, and even succumb to, most painful states of a traumatic character, in the sense that the quantity of excitation aroused may be beyond the infant's ability to master. Three possible sources of traumatization can be envisaged:

(1) *Increase of excitation (stimulation).* Teething is an example of increased excitation that arouses inner-perceptual activities with which the self has to deal by means of (a) negative hallucination, (withdrawal of cathexis from the sensation) which will be of short duration; (b) loss of oral sucking, activity and of appetite, which corresponds to withdrawal of cathexis of the organ and its accustomed activity (extinction of oral-erotic desires); (c) turning inward of oral aggression not utilized in the feeding process which is refused; (d) attempts at ego control of stimulation by biting the finger or hand with the gums, which are in fact attempts at integration of pain with the help of the hand; (e) failure of these attempts and cessation of self-control expressed in crying and convulsive activities.

The solutions found (a-c) may become paradigmatic for dealing with subsequent states of increased excitation (pathology of the body-ego).

(2) *Inadequacy of the self in dealing with excitation (stimulation).* The self emerges as a function of the interaction between inner drive (stimulation) and the apparatus (bodily organs like the mouth) through which the drive acts. Sometimes this interaction seems quiescent, though there are ample signs of the presence of stimulation. The instinctual drive meets a body and a self which respond only slowly. This may reflect a slight delay of ego development which need not be of any clinical significance. But it may also mean that ego deveopment has been so retarded as to have fallen out of step with instinctual development. Translated into the

teething period, it means that, while the teeth break through accompanied by a comparatively enormous increase of oral-sadistic stimulation, neither the stomach and intestinal apparatus nor the mouth, tongue, and hand have achieved the state of body-ego maturity needed to master this quantity of oral-sadistic excitation, in itself normal.

(3) *Failure of the "Not-Self."* By this I mean the defect or excess displayed by the nursing mother, who is called upon to remove what interferes with the quiet growth of the self until it turns to the object as such. From the point of view of the infant's inner economy this failure results either in an increase of excitation or in the self's becoming inadequate for dealing with normal excitation. Too little milk heightens the demand for abolishing hunger: enough food, enough intake, but inadequate administration does the same. In both conditions the infant will react as if only his inner excitation were raised. His capability of controlling excitation is low, but within its range the self makes use of the body and the apparatus as if it were acting thoughtfully and with foresight.

4

Mutual Influences
in the
of Ego and Id

I should like to narrow my task and concentrate on one aspect only, namely the earliest differentiation of id and ego. In doing so I shall not be in a position to contribute anything relevant from the clinical point of view. Mental functioning in its onset is too complex and controversial a subject to allow a satisfactory examination together with a simultaneous view of the clinical problems related to it.

Some discrepancy between clinical theory (psychopathology) and theory of early mental functioning is most likely to be felt when research work on the psychogenesis and psychoanalytic treatment of states like psychosis are under discussion. This has been recognized for some years past. In *Inhibition, Symptom and* examined the regressive processes which take place in early development and result in obsessional mechanisms, and he asked whether regression from the phallic to the anal-sadistic level of instinct transformation should perhaps be accounted for by—as he called it—a *time factor* and not by a *constitutional factor*, which would promote *fixation*. In Freud's words, "It may be that regression is rendered possible not because the genital organization of the libido is too weak but because the opposition of the ego begins too early, while the sadistic phase is at its height." Clinical thought since has frequently reoriented itself on facts and theories relating to the development of the young ego but no doubt the balance is still in favor of pure reconstruction of early mental life based on clinical impressions. Direct investigations and observations by psychoanalysts are still scanty; though very valuable in themselves, they are often overrated or too quickly made into generalizations. Today it can safely be assumed that a new generation of psychoanalysts will finally accept only those hypotheses relating to the onset of mental life which have been arrived at by a close confrontation of factual material concerning early development with hypotheses primarily derived from clinical experience.

What follows is merely a summary of such theoretical and empirical statements as underlie our present ideas on the early phases of id-ego development and differentiation.

THE DEVELOPMENTAL ASPECT OF THE ID

If the id can be conceived as rather immutable in its core, then the nearer it comes to the ego—its cortical layer—the more it appears to be plastic, colored by its objects, and beset with the consequences of functional changes, cathexes, and anticathexes. It is here, near its surface, that the developmental changes which we can safely attribute to the id manifest themselves. I mean, of course, the expression of the drives in terms of oral, anal, sadomasochistic, phallic, and genital organization. (Whenever possible, I shall speak of "instinctual drives," implying the fusion of aggressive and erotic instincts.)

According to Freud (1915c) the *object* of an instinct is that thing or person *in* or *through* which it can achieve its aim. "The object is the most variable thing about an instinct, is not originally connected with it, but becomes attached to it only in consequence of its being peculiarly fitted to provide satisfaction. The object is not necessarily an extraneous one; it may be part of the subject's own body. It may be changed any number of times in the course of the visissitudes the instinct undergoes during life; a highly important part is played by this capacity for displacement in the instinct" (p. 122).

Enough stress can never be laid on the distinction between the aim of a drive on the one hand, and the object "peculiarly fitted to provide satisfaction" on the other. It is therefore in accordance with contemporary psychoanalytic usage to say that the developmental aspect of the id does not reach beyond the progression from pregenitality to genitality. The ego and the id may originate in a common matrix but the fate of the two derivatives is different. While the development of the id ceases with the attainment of genitality, that of the ego continues through childhood and adolescence into adulthood.

THE BODY AS AN OBJECT OF THE ID DRIVES

The developmental aspect of the drives expressed in their progress through the different stages of pregenitality to genitality has steered us to a new mental structure, the *body-ego*. According to Freud's description the body has to be conceived as the instinct's object and at the same time as a device for discharge closest to the source of the instinct. Instincts as such do not know or tolerate postponement of discharge. They seek it in the object in or through which they can achieve their aim. They do not make their objects, they only make use of their availability. The "making of the objects" of the instincts in addition to what is there from the start, the body, is the result of the functioning of the ego.

INTERNAL MILIEU (INTERNAL ENVIRONMENT)

The ontogenesis of the ego is, as we know, one of the darkest chapters in psychoanalysis. In our ignorance of the origin of the instincts we have to resort to biology and biochemistry. We may say with Nunberg (1932) that the id has created its ego, but we should still like to know *how* it has done so. We can, however, see a little light if we conceive the body not only as the first object in which and *through* which an instinct seeks gratification but also as the object which lends itself in an instinct-regulating manner to this function.

Though the object is, as we have just said, interchangeable, it is contained in the body from the first moment that instincts come into operation. It provides psychologically Claude Bernard's *milieu interne,* the internal environment, which is created by the fact that instincts always flow out from a source to objects, in which they achieve their aim. The first psychological *milieu interne* of an ideal character is equated in our theory to *primary identification,* the functional aspect of *primary narcissism.* In her paper on "Affects in Theory and Practice," Marjorie Brierley (1951) said, "At the beginning of mental life we are accustomed to posit a phase, prior to object-differentiation and cathexis, that we label primary identification. This initial stage is by definition lacking in cognitive discrimination." Brierley thinks that *primary identification* "is presumed to be a state of feeling awareness" but that "it can scarcely be devoid of sensory impressions. The very ambiguity of the English word 'feeling' indicates that this state is a *fusion of sensory and affect awareness.*"

As examples to illustrate this primary identification Brierley cites, as Freud originally did, the infant's experiences with the mother's breast and its own mouth, whereas I should exemplify primary narcissism and identification by the infant's state of deep sleep. I assume that Bertram Lewin (1950) would do the same. What I mean is this; what happens in deep sleep we conjecture to be an almost complete withdrawal of cathexes. In it primary narcissism and identification—the lack of all qualities discriminating between self and not-self, inside and outside are temporarily achieved.

Sleep is interfered with at the beginning of life (where it is not yet conditioned by a preconscious sense of time) by instinctual needs which call for objects in or through which gratification can be secured. Any instinctual demand that arises during deep sleep—

including of course the demand for waking—will upset the state of primary narcissism and the "ideal internal milieu." Some of these urges find their objective immediately with the aid of the body apparatus. The act or urination, for instance, or finger sucking, or sucking of the lip or tongue, will relieve the need to discharge the urge, its *aim* being relief, some sensation of pleasure in or through the *object* in which the need was felt, that is, through parts of the infant's or fetus's body. In the case of micturition the sensory experience may extend over those parts of the body which become wet or cooler in consequence of evaporation, or it may cease altogether after micturition, when urine is soaked up by a diaper, and so on. In the sucking experience the sensation will be reinforced by not-body objects—the milk, the breast, the bottle, the mother's grip, breath or heartbeat.

When unpleasant sensations, some form of "pain" amounting to a "need" are felt, what apparatus is there to deal with them? I think at first none, except a biological (animal) "instinct" which works by motor discharges (Margaret Mahler's "affectomotor storm") which betray the absence of an organizing, synthesizing, integrating agency or ego. Such an "affectomotor storm" can be described in Freud's words (slightly modified) as the consequence of a departure from primary narcissism, leading to the body's vigorous attempt to recover it (1914c). *Organized* recoveries from unpleasant stimuli, built up step by step, are first and foremost drawn from the infant's own body and are only possible with the help of *memory traces* (Glover, 1950). Thinking therefore in terms of simultaneous experiences of sensations aroused inside and outside the feelings in the course of instinct gratification should lead to a reinforcement and temporary extension of the sensation of the self.

The more one thinks of young infants, their earthquakelike reactions to pain (which upsets the state of primary narcissism and defies primary identification) and of their initial indifference to stimulation from outside (before this becomes the source of pleasure), the more one is inclined to assume that "self" and "me" experiences are called upon to operate; they tend either to *preserve* or, if lost, in an attack of pain, to *restore* the inner equilibrium. The only mechanisms I can conceive as achieving this effect at this stage are those of negative and positive hallucination.

THE PROBLEM OF HALLUCINATION
IN EARLY INFANCY

The concept of negative hallucination was mentioned on a few occasions by Freud, mainly descriptively, but in one instance he seemed to accord it a high theoretical value. "Any attempt to explain hallucination," he said, "would have to be made from the starting-point of a negative hallucination, rather than from a positive one" (1917, p. 232). He did not, accordingly, refer to "primary repression" when mentioning "negative hallucination."

Positive hallucination has been readily accepted and used by psychoanalysts, including Freud himself, in explaining the infant's first attempts at need fulfillment, but its negative counterpart has not. Negative hallucination we can conceive as a kind of sensory and affective deafness. It may at first be invoked against the disturbing influence of inner stimuli, and it functions to raise the physiological threshold of stimulation. When we fall asleep we sometimes have to make a definitve effort to withdraw from the stimuli which still reach our outer and inner sense organs; we have to use shutters to keep out awareness of any change, inside or outside, which would otherwise lead to stimulation and reaction. This we achieve with the help of repression. Negative hallucination means that a stimulus does not reach the sensory system. Perhaps it is not more than an effect of mobile energy which just balances the stimulus. Freud has commented on the work of mobile cathexis in a passage which, so far as I know, has not yet been integrated into contemporary psychoanalytic thinking, but has recently been emphasized in the work of Hartmann, Kris and Loewenstein. In the third appendix to *Inhibition, Symptom and Anxiety* (1926, p. 171) Freud says:

When there is physical pain a high degree of what may be termed narcissistic cathexis of the painful place occurs. This cathexis continues to increase and tends, as it were, to empty the ego. It is well known that when internal organs are giving pain, spatial and other images of the affected part of the body arise, though that part is not represented in conscious ideation on other occasions. In contrast to that, when the mind is diverted to some other interest by psychological means, even the most intense physical pains fail to arise. (I must not say "remain unconscious" in this case.) This remarkable truth can be accounted for by the fact that there is a concentration of cathexis on the psychical representative of the part of the body which is giving pain.

It has obviously been easier for psychoanalysts to accept the concept of positive hallucination. In infant psychology it has been used to explain the affective experience of need fulfillment in a non-real manner, as if the instinctual drive had reached its aim on the body organ in conjunction with a hallucinated, not an existent object, say the breast or the milk. Positive hallucinations dealing with the infant's hunger phenomena are always transient; other hallucinations may definitely pacify less vital instinctual needs more permanently.

Negative and positive hallucinations therefore work in the service of instinctual gratification and for the acquiescence of the self in this process. Both forms of hallucination restore, at least for a while, the internal equilibrium or homeostasis. In *positive hallucination* the absent part-object of the instinct has definitely undergone a change—temporary of course—as if it were there and gave satisfaction. But this is hardly conceivable without postulating some kind of *memory trace*. And such traces must arise from some experience of physical reality. (As Freud tells us, *some* element of truth is generally operative in all delusions.) Postive hallucinations, then, can be conceived of only in an infant who has already experienced physical gratifications of the kind which are now hallucinated. Since they are related to memory traces, some kind of functioning ego has to be in operation as well.

If we think of the reasons put forward by Freud when he said the dream is a psychosis, there is no objection to our saying that in certain infantile situations of need we conjecture that postponement of gratification is tolerated only by the aid of a psychotic mechanism.

ORAL PRIMACY AND OBJECT

The progressive cathexis of the body is brought about in two ways, leading to a form of oral primacy: first, by intensified oral stimulation, and second, by progressive differentiation of the oral-intestinal apparatus followed by improving oral mastery of needs encroaching on the self (development of the body ego).

By intensified oral stimulation nothing else can be meant but the effect of motherly care. It is not solely the consequence of the mother's acceptance of her child. It is rooted in the child's need for more food, more attention, in consequence of its fast-growing, demanding body and therefore in consequence of its lesser need for sleep. Here factors of maturation enter the picture, leading to the subsequent enrichment of the inner milieu, the *"inner world of the infant"* by the memory traces and the actual pleasant experiences resulting from better instinctual channeling and control (avoidance of unpleasure and pain). The step to the psychological object, which now comes into existence irrespective of its physical presence or absence, has been taken.

We now must conceive of an ego's object: it is something or someone that is desired, draws cathexis away from the body, can be looked at, and progressively becomes separated from the exciting emotions (affects) and from the body-self experiences in the feeding and nursing situation. To the extent that memory is already functioning, it allows for very fine discrimination; but I do not think we can say yet at which level of early ego organization the discrimination between *individuals*, offering themselves as objects, can be conceived to operate. In the past, psychoanalysts seem to have placed these processes too late. Interest in the pioneer work of Ferenczi and his school, predominantly by Alice and Michael Balint, and the work of Anna Freud, Spitz, Ribble, Greenacre, and Bowlby, has already led to some modification of our timetable, while the work of Melanie Klein hypothesizes discriminating faculties in the infant from the very onset of life.

SLEEP AND WAKEFULNESS

The infant's object relationship, once in being, is annulled and recreated psychologically and physically in rhythmic periods indicated by sleep and wakefulness. Perhaps the mental experiences associated with awakening are as important as those related to feeding and nursing in our ealiest unconscious experiences. Psychologically the acts leading to awakening must be considered as body-self experiences, an aspect elaborated by Paul Federn (1932). Bodily sensations in the state of awakening are "me-experiences." They ensue after the gratifying need for sleep has been fulfilled. Here no one can do more than describe impressions gained by chance observation, since no one has examined this field with the eyes of a psychoanalyst so as to be able to offer us a more elaborate vista. We know, of course, that awakening is never merely the consequence of sleep-need-gratification. In very early life, however, (fetal and neonatal), an active aggressive longing for contact with a self, with objects and the outer world is difficult to conceive: this need has to be *created*. I think this conjecture will be verifiable when the incubator, in which the prematurely born are nursed and fed, becomes the place for observation. Then we shall be in a better position to understand how far the sleep-waking rhythm, in psychological terms the state of primary narcissism and identification and the ego's "vigorous attempts" to recover it, are part of an autonomous ego in the sense suggested by Hartmann. In the future, such autonomous factors can no longer be neglected.

The suggestion that we watch the infant's waking from sleep or even the prematurely born in its incubator can be considered what E. Kris (1951) termed "action research." Its results will not be confined to what passive observation (the behaviorist's "pure research") reveals, but will depend on the observer's first intuitive understanding and reaction to the total situation observed.

Examples of such understanding, based on empathy with the early mother-child relationship, are found in the work of D.W. Winnicott (1951).

SELF AND OBJECT

I believe, however, that as a consequence of our knowledge of the effects of deprivation in early infancy, we have now approached a stage in our applied child psychology where we interpret onesidedly the infant's growing inner need to establish an object relationship, emphasizing his helplessness rather than his developing capacities. The emptying of the preconscious and unconscious of the cathexes—object, self, body—is of course not confined to the biological rhythms of sleep; it operates for instance in fainting, in convulsions, and above all in the infant's state of *psychological helplessness* (M.S. Mahler's "organismic distress," 1952). Such states are more characteristic of the undifferentiated state of the id-ego relationship than of any later stage of ego development. They may occur without the noisy concomitants of the traumatic event of birth or of later traumas suffered by the active child; they may be "silent traumas."

These states of helplessness as such are not the subject under discussion there. What we cannot omit when discussing the earliest influences id and ego may exert on each other is the query: What are the psychological events which cause the helpless infant's body, his self, and the objects which have just entered into his life to be recathected? As in the state of gradual awakening, what still puzzles us are the methods which are employed to recover the state of *pretraumatic organization,* faint and fragile as it is. How does the constant flow of instincts lead to the recovery of the self and do there remain residues, *loci minoris resistentiae*? Do they become reenacted in the ego-dissociating events of later life, clinically called psychotic states and episodes?

We are not yet in a position to answer these questions, but we can relate the recovery from a state of helplessness to the infant's object relationship. I think we can assume that the infant's *sensitivity* to pain and unpleasure, its tolerance of anxiety is gradually conditioned by the number, length, and depth of the states of helplessness through which it passes (Greenacre, 1952). Its traumatized body as such does not easily provide the amount of stimulation of body-ego experiences for which the growing and recovering self longs. The self is not regained, I assume, without the help of the objects. The mechanism for achieving this recovery is introjection as an instinct gratificaiton which, according to Hartmann, is the forerunner of introjection as a defense mechanism. We cannot at this stage think of introjection as gratification *and* defense, as Joan Riviere (1936) has described it, or of projection, which, according to Glover (1939), is regarded by some observers as characteristic of the mental apparatus from its earliest beginnings. With the aid of introjection the infant builds up again its narcissistic equilibrium and restores its "protective barrier." This process leads to secondary narcissism and thus paves the way for future genuine investments in the objects of the outer world. Self-control through object-control finally leads to transient object love.

CONCLUSION

I have sought for two reasons to trace the mutual influences in the development of the ego and the id back to the earliest stages of infantile life: first, because a reorientation of the infant's psychology has been tried for quite a number of years by psychoanalysts and the only comprehensive reconstruction so far, the work of Melanie Klein (1948) and her co-workers, has in my opinion not taken fully into account the wealth of Freud's heritage on the one hand and of more recent child psychological research on the other. In this respect it is still oriented on the integrative endeavours of the late Susan Isaacs. Second, Hartmann, Kris, and Loewenstein's formulations of an undifferentiated phase now allow for a better explanation of the basic properties of the ego and the id. It deserves special emphasis that Hartmann has just put forward all evidence available at this juncture for assuming that the basic functions of the ego (control and perception, motility, memory, experience and learning) are not *created* by the needs, they are only *developed* under their influence: in fact they are inborn and their deveopment, as he says, follows "certain laws, which are also part of our inheritance." From what he says I can deduce that psychic reality results primarily from the interaction of the drives with the inherited apparatus, secondarily from the interaction of both with the outer world. What I myself have to add is that the processes leading to ego-id differentiation originate in the infant's body and that no environment exists until the self as a "me-experience" has come into existence. By these means the body, as Freud has stated, attains a special position among other objects in the world of perception. Instinct and ego maturation is also reflected in body-ego maturation. Even though the environment may by and large deal successfully with the infant's needs, many situations of stress amounting to a loss of the feeling of self must still arise. I am inclined to believe that this loss is re-created in a more arduous way than we may imagine in the earliest acts of awakening. I am disposed further to believe that in the infant's frequently posited *inertia* there is an active element which may be likened to Freud's concept of negative hallucination. The situations of inner stress may amount to traumas, and these may lead to the first anticipation of the affect of anxiety. The environment plays an active part in the mastery of this anxiety though it cannot entirely prevent it. From the occurrence of traumas and anxiety I deduce that an active drive toward the objects in the outer world emerges— a drive which of course at this stage is at the service of the oral partial instinct. With it, the first object relationship ensues. A partial differentiation of the id and what there is of an ego has taken place.

I am reminded here of what Anna Freud (1951) has called "telescoping." She said that our work with our patients deals with single events of the past which in fact turn out to be a long series of events; that the highly charged emotional experiences which they report and relieve are in fact condensations (primary process) of numerous affects of childhood which, to an adult witness, would seem small, indeed almost insignificant. Our individual histories would have to be drawn out at interminable length if they were to approximate to what really happened. It would, however, take too long to listen to them. In trying to present in relief a contemporary understanding of the first months of life I have done nothing more than try to undo some of the telescoping we have done in our various theories of earliest infancy.

5

The Earliest Phases
of Ego Development

This work is not directly concerned with psychiatry as such but aims at penetrating into those phases of early mental development which we now think have a bearing on the etiology of psychoses.

At the turn of the century, in his pioneering studies into the etiology and treatment of neuroses, Freud conceived behavior, both overt and implicit, as the resultant of two sets of forces: the forces of drive and the forces of defense. To begin with, it was the forces of drive, or instinct, which captured his attention. Thus, in his classical monograph "Three Essays on the Theory of Sexuality" (1905) he made a detailed examination of the nature of the sexual instinct, and of the vicissitudes it underwent during its development toward maturity. He outlined the forms which sexuality assumes in childhood, its aims, the range of its possible objects, and the characteristics of discharge of instinctual tension. He demonstrated the transformation of the biologically rooted drives into a wide variety of behavior. Thus he was able to comprehend within the framework of a unified theory the hitherto little-related facts of sexual perversion, of sadism and masochism, of exhibitionism and scoptophilia, of homosexuality and also of child behavior, of adult neuroses, and of normal adult sexual life. He could show how, in a neurosis, symptoms were developed as compromise formations in a struggle against the expression of the very impulses and desires that the pervert reveals so freely. For instance, he could show an identity of motivaiton in cases of overt homosexuality and in those of paranoia where a system of delusions was built up to ward off homosexual wishes. Again, an identity of motivating forces could be shown to exist in exhibitionism and in agoraphobia, in both of which being looked at is so important—in the one as a wish, in the other as a dread. Further, the passionate curiosity of voyeurism, when prohibited, could play its part in the development of learning inhibitions. To use a metaphor, some of the perversions and neuroses could be paired off and located as the positive and negative poles of the same field of force.

The reconciliation of these apparent opposites was effected by means of a theory which took account of the common instinctual basis of these contrasting types of behavior. Thus it was natural that at first, stress should be laid upon the prime importance of these common features. But, as analytic experience and research progressed, the time came for a more detailed examination of the defensive functions, of the barriers which grew up in the path of the instinctual drives, of those forces, now called "ego-forces" which transformed the common bases into specific personal, individual features. At first, it was the crippling effects of the defensive functions which called for attention: the absorption of the obsessive compulsive patient's sexual energy into the rituals he performed against that sexuality; the completeness with which the hysterical conversions and phobias took the place of love relationships. Such compromise formations also showed how economically the mental apparatus performed its work, since, in the distortion of symptoms, both the warded-off and forbidden sexual or aggressive wish and the punishment for it could be discerned.

As analytic studies progressed, more came to be known of the defensive processes defined by Freud as early as 1905 as "the psychic correlates of the flight reflex which follow the task of guarding against the origination of pain from inner sources." The pathological effect of the defensive processes in neurotic symptom formation has to be understood, however, as only a special instance of ego functioning. From the year 1920 onward the concept of defense had to be widened beyond that developed from the field of psychopathology. The concept of the ego and the understanding of the variety of mechanisms which it uses in mediating between inner sources of tension (i.e., the instinctual drives and outer reality) has come to have equal importance in analytic thinking with the theory of the instinctual drives. To this development we owe much to Anna Freud who in "The Ego and the Mechanisms of Defense" (1937) opened the way to a new clinical understanding of ego functioning.

That this aspect of theory should develop later than that of instincts is understandable if we consider that the two sets of forces—instinctual drives and regulating, channelling ego forces—are more readily distinguished when they are in conflict than when they work in harmony. If ego functioning proceeds without opposition toward the goal of obtaining satisfaction for the id, and if achieves this goal in a way that is congruent with social reality, then it is hard to distinguish the two components, drives and ego, in what becomes an harmonious function.

Given evidence for the operation of common drives in all human beings, we nevertheless can observe that there is an enormous range of variation between people. If we think of instinctual drives as Freud did (1915)—as a quasi-biological concept, representing a demand on the mental apparatus for work—then we may attribute variation, namely that resulting from the *interaction* of the first two, drive and apparatus. This third source, the interactive source of variation, is the ego, a developing psychological structure dependent for its power on the other two sources, but coincident or identical with neither of them.

In the observation of children, some notable attempts have been made in the United States to assess variations in the strength of the instinctual drives and in their precocity. Some workers assume that ego variations in small children could be accounted for by quantitative differences in the individual instinctual drives. For instance, Fries and Woolf (1953), in their work of distinguishing between different "activity types" among young infants, have made valuable contributions toward the solution of this problem. Some children are very much more active and aggressive in their responses to stimulation than others. They in turn call down upon themselves more restrictive control from their environment than do the placid infants who sleep more and move less or grasp and even press the nipple less forcefully.. Other studies have concentrated on early manifestations of adaptive ego functions themselves. A growing body of evidence points to marked and early demonstrated differences among children in their capacity to deal with new stimulus-situations. Again, there would appear to be considerable variability in the kind of situations which arouse tension in different infants, as Leitch and Escalona (1950) have shown in their studies of infants' reactions to stress. Careful follow-up studies based on this kind of infant-observation should be able to contribute in an important degree to our understanding of the interplay between drives, ego, and environment.

When we consider the nature of the environment—the reality to which the child adapts himself and upon which he is initially dependent for his instinctual satisfaction but over which he gradually comes to effect some active control—we find that we need to distinguish between the world of things and the world of people. Further, there is one area of his social reality which stands in a quite special relation to other realities. This is the sphere of the self, that which brings about the feeling of *myself* in contrast to things and objects.

We can readily see how things come to be treated as people. Winnicott (1953) describes the development of "transitional objects," toys and blankets, or sometimes articles of clothing that come to have an intense emotional meaning for the young child, as symbols of the people to whom he has become closely attached. Laura, the subject of Robertson's film (1952) clung to and used her Teddy bear and blankets as we suspect she wanted to use her mother. It is harder to see how the *self* is treated as an object, another person, at that early age. As I shall show presently, it is not easy to avoid this issue. Many problems of adaptation to the world at large can be better understood if we try to trace the reciprocal relation between reactions to other people and things on the one hand, and reaction to the self on the other. The self as a field of stimulation and response takes part in some degree in all experiences and, in the course of development, becomes progressively more important as a stable focus of interaction. In other words, the self is a "constant" in all interchange with the environment. When it loses this constancy, when it disintegrates, the perception of, and the relationship with the environment disintegrates and psychosis-like states result.

First, let us look at some of the relations between the characteristics and the quality of the child's reaction to the environment and his developing relation to himself. The first observations we can make of the child's relation to himself are those of his reaction to his own body (Hoffer, 1949, 1950). In these reactions we can discern an early differentiation on the infant's body surface: the differentiation of a feeling of inner need, the demand of the instinctual drive, from the feeling of self, conveyed to the child through his early primitive ego functions. Our clue to this differentiation of psychic structure is to be found in the *voluntary, intentional* use of one part of the body to allay tension arising in another part. I am thinking here of the situation, which does not usually arise before the twelfth week, when, no longer reflexively but quite intentionally, the hand is put into the mouth to relieve oral tension. In this act of voluntary motor control, by which two sensations—oral and tactile—are simultaneously aroused, the child succeeds in obtaining an autoerotic satisfaction of the oral partial instinct. That is, he uses one function—motor control—to effect a reduction in tension arising from within the body. He uses one part of himself to satisfy another part. The hand serves the need for oral-pleasure sucking, while the breast or bottle of course serve the need for sucking *and* for food. It is of great interest to observe how, from the twelfth week onward or even earlier, the hand helps in the feeding process by being placed on the breast or bottle. From 16 weeks onward a more definite grasping response may occur when the infant, on seeing the bottle, grasps it as it is brought to the mouth and may hold his hand or hands firmly around the bottle or breast.

In the course of observations reported elsewhere (Hoffer, 1949) I found the most striking fact in the sucking behavior of infants to be the directness and resolution with which, from the twelfth week onward, the infant made his fingers approach his mouth. This can be observed at any time during waking hours but is accentuated before and after feeding. The hand may be introduced by the shortest route or by a wide circle, while the eyes may follow the movements of the hand, the thing in front of the baby's field of vision. In infants of that age I could seldom observe vigorous sucking movements when the fingers entered the mouth, which was contrasted rather strongly to the response of the infant in need of food when the bottle was brought to the mouth. The finger sucking is a rhythmic, intensive, and pleasurable sucking process. Most striking was the response of Tom, for instance, whom I filmed: at 16 weeks old, he showed unusual effort and exertion. He held his arms slightly bent in front of his face, his fingers were stretched out, and those of one hand tried to grasp the thumb of the other with a pincer movement. While both hands tried to get closer to each other with jerky movements, Tom's mouth was kept open; he made an effort as if he were trying to lift his head from the pillow and his lips sucked in air like a turbine. When he succeeded in catching his thumb and introducing it into his mouth, his left hand was held over his mouth, locking it and preventing his right hand from sliding out again. If it did slide out, his left hand quickly pushed it back again, up toward the palate, accompanied by quite intensive sucking for a 16-weeks-old infant.

(Gesell and Ilg (1937) say of the 16-weeks-old baby that he brings his fingers together over his chest and engages them in mutual finger play. His fingers finger his fingers. Thus he touches himself and is touched simultaneously. This double touch of hand on hand and hand on mouth is a lesson in self-discovery. He comes to appreciate what his fingers are, and that things and objects around him are something different from his fingers.

This process by which the infant becomes able to use part of himself as a substitute source of satisfaction develops out of the hunger response. He learns thereby the distinction between self and not-self, things and potential objects. This process can be considered the prototype of all "self"; the skills which were practiced in self-stimulation and self-satisfaction are transferred a little later to objects external to the infant. Thus Tom, in grasping one hand with the other, was learning a skill whaich he was to transfer some weeks later to the grasping of inanimate objects.

In behavior like this I believe we can see a nucleai ego which displays those ego functions described by Freud in his first formulation (1923), including:

1. *Genuine percentual activity.* The infant of three months upward sees his hand, focuses on it, follows its movements with his eyes. In the setting described there is true perception of a thing outside. There is no longer the close primal relationship between sight and mere movement.

2. *Motor control.* The movements of the hand toward the mouth are achieved in spite of great difficulties of an ataxia-like character. The infant counteracts such ataxia; he tries to aid the hand which is to be sucked. Mouth and hand combine in a pleasurable realization of the space which is within the reach of arms, hands, and mouth. The mouth ego has widened to the space embraced by the arms.

3. *Functioning of memory.* This is suggested by the repetition of a specific mode of gratification. Out of a vast free choice of possible positions of hand and fingers, the infant develops and adheres to a limited number of sucking patterns.

4. *Reality testing.* This can be traced in the infant's meticulous choice of what he wishes to introduce into his mouth. When he wishes to introduce his fingers, he will easily reject, as far as his powers allow, the spoon, comforter, or breast. Insofar as the infant learns to distinguish between inner wishes and the sources of gratification—i.e., hallucinatory versus real gratification (see Freud, 1911, 1917)—his adaptation to and control of outer reality will improve.

The association of hand and mouth may become so close that it can temporarily interfere with the feeding process and the feeding function of the mouth. The infant may insist either on sucking his fingers at the same time as he is being fed or refuse to be fed at all because of his wish to suck only his fingers. While Gesell records this observation as if it were an accidental interference with the feeding process caused by the hand, our Hampstead Nurseries film leads us to interpret this behavior as *competition* between the feeding process and the finger-sucking.

The necessity felt by mothers of holding the hands down to prevent fingers and breast (or bottle or spoon) from being sucked at the same time, as Gesell states, has probably obscured this competitive behavior on the part of the infant. However, Winnicott (1945) mentions that "some babies put a finger in the mouth while sucking the breast, thus (in a way) holding on to self-created reality while using external reality." This behavior could quite frequently be observed in infants from about the fourteenth week onward. In one case the infant adds his thumb to the bottle in the mouth and insists on its remaining there while he is fed; in another case he tolerates the bottle well without interfering by finger-sucking but starts to introduce the finger immediately when fed spinach with a spoon.

Let us now consider the relation between this self-development in the area of "appetitive" behavior and those responses which are homeostatic in a different sense: the avoidance responses, not connected with pleasure or pain. By virtue of his nervous and motor structure, and child is capable from birth onward of both approach and avoidance responses. Initially these function in the most primitve way only, with all the lack of specificity characteristic of early "mass action."

It was Freud (1925) who suggested that the first differentiation which the infant makes is between pleasurable good things, which are conceived as part of the self, and the unpleasant things which are not part of the self. The differentiation comes about in consequence of the signals received through the sensory system, at first mainly through the mouth, which is the first and foremost sense organ to function. But in addition we have to think of another differentiating system in the body, that between "pain" and "not pain." The infant learns when communicating with the world at large, which for him need not yet be a world separated from his own self, that he has to take into account the "pain barrier." This barrier plays its paramount role only after free movement sets in, but from early infancy onward it is a very potent safeguard against the turning of the aggressive instinct, exemplified by the muscular apparatus, against the infant's own body. When reality testing is learned, the pain barrier (Hoffer, 1950b, 1950a) plays its part; and when the barrier is neglected, traumatic, painfully damaging experiences ensue. These will be followed by protective measures, by anxiety and inhibition of function, by withdrawal or arrest of discharge, by accumulation of aggression, by rage or attack, but hardly by self-destructiveness. The pain barrier will oppose this and, if it fails to do so, will herald severe abnormality.

This aspect of the pain barrier in its relation to self-destructiveness has so far received little attention in the vast literature on the subject of pain. As the famous biologist, Von Uexkuell said in his "Theoretical Biology" (1926, p. 145):

Pain forms one of the most powerful indications of the subject's own body, and its chief duty is to prevent self-mutilation. So it imposes a strong check which shall prevent, in all circumstances, the continuation of any initiated action that is hurtful to the body. This is especially necessary in the case of carnivorous animals: rats, for instance, will immediately devour their own legs, if the sensory nerves to these have been servered. Now in many animals a tendency to self-mutilation is a fundamental arrangement in their organization, serving to save the whole body by the sacrifice of imperilled limbs. In such animals, the action of pain as a check to the reflex would merely be an inconvenience, and so we may assume that it is not there. Moreover in some cases where there is no tendency to self-mutilation, it can be shown directly that there is no pain, for even when the body is being injured there is no check set up. You can put the hind end of the big brown dragon fly between its own jaws, and see how it proceeds to chew its own body. Most of the lower animals are so constructed that they are never in danger of injuring their own bodies. When that does not occur, however, as in the sea-urchin, I have been able to show that there is a special arrangement, which I called *autodermophily* and this takes the place of pain. The skin of these animals secretes a substance that prevents the normal reflex of snapping by the pedicellariae. Amoebae are able to distinguish the pseudopodia of their own body from those of other individuals. What this depends on we cannot determine. The conditions are reversed here from what they are in other animals. Since they have no framework which can be injured by their eating themselves, it is quite in order for them to be perpetually ingesting their own protoplasm. So that, in their case, pain would make their very existence problematical. Pain certainly does not play the absolutely senseless role usually ascribed to it, of transforming the whole living world into a vale of misery and fear. Pain is present only where there is a place for it in the plan of the organism, and where, consequently, it is necessary and useful.

In the infant the operation of the pain barrier, which initially serves to some degree as a protection against self-hurt or self-destructiveness, is reinforced by a progressive libidinization of the body, the beginning of which I indicated when discussing the funtion of finger sucking. The mouth-self which the infant succeeds in creating gradually expands to the body-self. In his self the infant finds a substitute for the first close attachment to the mother from which he must gradually be weaned. That is, he comes to love himself with part of the love which at first was totally absorbed in his relations with his mother. And because he loves himself he deflects his aggressive, destructive reactions away from himself. We may assume, then, that the self regulates and spreads instinctual tensions, aggressive and erotic alike. This double protection against self-destructiveness—the pain barrier and self-regard—explains the intensity of aggressiveness turned outward against the outer world and the increase of self-love, of narcissistic feelings, if this form of mastery is successful. Infantile narcissism is thus a protection against self-inflicted pain, though not against dangers from outside or accidents.

Confirmation of this view if found in negative observations: in the fact that when the stage of teething and biting is at its height, during the second half of the first year and the first half of the second, it rarely happens that a child bites his own hand, though he may often fail to keep his balance and may drop the food just as the fingers have been put into the mouth. Although bodily injury is only too frequent at this stage—if the child is given a fair opportunity to move about—the teeth are rarely the cause of self-injury, though biting may be practiced on toys, on the cot, and on the mother herself. We may say that the child who likes himself will not bite himself.

When we come across cases of self-biting we are justified in our suspicion that they represent either an asymbolia of pain (Rubins et al., 1948) or a psychopathological development with the sensory apparatus unimpaired. We had an opportunity at the Hampstead War Nurseries (directed by Dorothy Burlingham and Anna Freud) of observing such a case. (Winnicott, 1945). In December 1941 an infant girl, three and a half months old, was admitted, together with her mother, to the residential Hampstead War Nurseries and stayed there—with one interruption of nine months duration—until the age of three and a half years. She was the illegitimate child of a manic-depressive mother and an unknown soldier. The baby was breast-fed at the time of entering the nurseries, and breast-feeding continued until she was ten months old. For some periods an attempt was made to substitute a bottle for a breast feeding, sometimes with success. The infant's weight was 5½ lbs. at birth; it doubled after four months and trebled after eight months. On admission the baby vomited frequently and the time of taking her at the breast had to be shortened to ten minutes for each feeding, when vomiting stopped. Weight, however, was gained and lost again for no obvious reason. I mention these dates since some workers may feel inclined to see a relation between these early feeding disturbances and the later oral-aggressive behavior.

After some weeks of observation, signs of physical and mental retardation became more and more apparent. While the development of bodily function was steady though slow, both bodily skills and social responses were subject to sudden changes and variations. For some periods the girl remained unaffected by her mother's very obvious changes of mood; on other occasions she reacted very quickly by screaming. At the age of six months when the mother tried to give her a bottle she turned her head away and refused to take it; subsequently she started to bite her own hands and later bit her hands most violently with visible effect. When, at nine months, the mother worried whether or not she should start weaning, the baby bit the breast, refused it, and smacked it with her fists. She then took food well from a spoon; at other times she refused it altogether and took only liquids. Screaming and spitting were the signs of refusal. Later, after the first birthday, the slowness of her movements spread to the feeding process itself, and for long periods she seemed to fall asleep while being fed.

From eleven months onward her reactions to her mother's changing moods became definite. Often when her mother was in an excited state, the infant reacted with screaming. When one year and two months old she started to rock and stare at a point; this was very characteristic of her later behavior.

At the age of one year and seven months she had to go through a severe crisis. She had just succeeded in saying "Mummy" in addition to her only other word, "No," when her mother's condition deteriorated to such a degree that temporary confinement in a mental hospital was necessary. This meant separation from the daughter for about two months. Prior to this the girl had displayed head banging which became worse at night. Sometimes the banging was accompanied by smiles and pleasure, sometimes by screaming, and sometimes by silence.

Shortly after the mother's return from the mental hospital the girl contracted ringworm, at the age of one year and ten months. During the mother's absence the child had shown signs of progressive development, had started to play with other children and to chew her fingers instead of sucking them. She had to be moved to a special hospital set up under wartime conditions for the treatment of ringworm.

The time in hospital must have been a very unhappy one; it lasted for nine months, including a period of quarantine for scarlet fever. After her return from hospital, at the age of two years and seven months, she refused solid food and did not take it herself when left alone. For periods she had to be fed by force. She bit her hands and arms, which had to be kept bandaged to protect them. She cried incessantly for long periods and knocked her head quite forcefully against the wall, but two months later she did not need bandages and ate everything. Some time later she again began to bite herself still more violently without any traceable cause. There was a short period in which she would pinch her mother and other adults who entered her room, but eventually social withdrawal with merely negative reaction to anyone, even her mother, became the rule. She refused food, lost weight, and finally was accepted in a hospital for mental defectives under the Mental Deficiency Act. There her development took quite a favorable course, within the limits of mental defectiveness. She has ceased to bite herself except occasionally when here mother visits her. At present, at the age of 12 years, her condition is the same.

Observations like these corroborate the claim that strong and vehement aggressive strivings operate in the child during his early years and have to be dealt with by him. One may point to two forces lacking in the case described but operating in normal development: self-love and self-protection. In this case a constitutional factor must have been involved, expressing itself in the general retardation and near standstill of motor and psychic development, for instance, in the intelligence level; this deficit interacted with an environmental factor, the inadequacy and traumatic nature of the child-mother relationship. This leads me to stress again the reciprocal nature of the interaction between the developing self and its relation to objects. The basis for self-love rests in a good relationship with the mother. Inevitably, however hard she may try, the earliest love object cannot provide instantaneous and full satisfaction for the developing infant, and so delay and deprivation play their part as instigators to the seeking of satisfaction through the self. How far this is possible will depend on the quality of the maturing adaptive capacities and the quantitiative balance between indulgence and deprivation afforded by the environment.

The effect of this developing self-love (counteracting self-hate and fear of loneliness) is clear when we consider that the child who can love himself needs less from the mother and can tolerate a measure of deprivation and delay in his instinctual gratification. If the child has achieved this degree of self-love there is also no need for his aggression to turn against his mother, and it will not be intensified to the degree that he cannot accept anything that she may be able to offer him. It is my belief that in temper tantrums and in psychogenic fits, self-love and object-love have ceased to operate; in them aggression has got loose and flooded the whole ego-organization. Another outcome of reaction to deprivation which is sudden and intense, when the child has not matured sufficiently to react in any but the most primitive way, is the mobilization of aggression to such a degree that a grossly serious break occurs in the relationship with the mother. This may lead to depression-like reactions of hatred against the self. Studies of children suffering from the effect of separation from the mother substantiate this observation.

Parallel with the development of the self new features arise in the child's relation to his love-object. At first the mother has meaning for the infant only insofar as she can serve the need for tension reduction. Indeed we can say that during the early stages of childhood, for some time the object has no independent existence but is treated as part of the "milieu interne," serving the satisfaction of the child's inner needs in the way these needs are served by his own body. We may assume that the impact of the drives, or of the needs which represent them, is most imperative at the beginning of mental life, at the time when the ego organization is still minimal. While the child is under the full impact of these drives he demands from the object one thing only: immediate satisfaction. An object which cannot fulfill this requirement at a given moment cannot be maintained as such, and is exchanged for a more satisfactory one. Somewhat surprisingly, the same process has been found to occur in certain forms of delinquency in children and adolescents. These findings, mainly put forward by August Aichhorn (1935), have contributed much to our present understanding of pathological object-relationships.

The needs have to lessen in strength or be brought under ego control before nonsatisfying, e.g., absent, objects can retain their meaning for the child. This is where studies of separation between mother and child can help us. In the earliest months of life it seems possible to exchange the object—a psychological fact which is relevant when we consider adoption—provided the form of need satisfaction remains unaltered. Later, approximately at the age of 5 months, the personal attachment to the object increases in importance. It is then possible to vary the *form* of satisfaction provided the object remains the same. Thus the object has come to play an important role in the transformation and sublimation of instinctual demands. (Burlingham, 1944). During the period from 5 to 24 months, separation from the object causes intense distress because the child is so exclusively dominated by his needs that he cannot maintain his attachment to a non-satisfying object for more than a given period, varying from several hours to several days. After this interval, which is most upsetting for the child, need satisfaction is more readily accepted from, and attachment transfered to a substitute. As the ego matures, the child gradually develops the ability to retain object relationships of a positive, loving kind, during separations of increasing length.

As he grows older, the progressively more adaptive ego functions make possible increased mastery of the environment, but the child continues to take over in his reactions to himself what he experiences in his relations with objects and, conversely, to transfer to his objects what he has experienced with himself. As Burlingham and Anna Freud (1944) have noted in their observations of children's behavior:

The infant plays with the mother in the same ways in which he plays with himself. He pulls her hair, pokes his fingers into her eyes, her nose, mouth and ears, or plays with her fingers; similarly he plays with his own face and with his own hands. Pleasure is evidently gained both from his own body and from the mother's. Sometimes, in such a search for pleasure, the two are used in turn.

An example of this unity of body between child and motherly person is observed under nursery conditions as well.

Example. Rose had always, since babyhood, sucked her thumb before falling asleep. At 21 months she began the following bedtime plays with her favourite nurse. For several days she put her hand in the nurse's mouth and then fell asleep. In a next phase she would try to take the nurse's hand in her mouth. She would open it wide to get in as much of the big hand as possible. Another evening she was sucking her thumb in the usual way. Suddenly she nodded her head, took a corner of her blanket (the same corner which she always used to grasp tightly during thumb-sucking), tried to push it into the nurse's mouth, smiled contentedly and fell asleep.

This interchange between the object and the self represents a transitional stage in the development from the use of the object for need satisfaction to what is called "object constancy" (Hartmann, Hoffer, Anna Freud, 1952). "Object constancy" must be considered the last and most mature stage in the development of object relationships, and has a special bearing on the fate of the aggressive and hostile drives. In the state of "object constancy" the love object will not be rejected or exchanged for another if it cannot provide immediate and total satisfaction. It has ceased to be closely linked with the bodily needs, whose place in fact it has partly taken. In the state of "object constancy" the absent object is still longed for and not rejected (hated) as unsatisfactory.

In conclusion, perhaps we should regard the interplay between self and object as the central paradox of emotional development: this is that the child needs his mother's love in order to be able to love himself, in order to be able to do without her love, so that he is ultimately able to love another person as he was loved by his mother.

6

The Psychoanalytic Investigation of Childhood, with Special Reference to Problems of Childhood Illness

In its relation to general psychiatry, child psychiatry is approaching a state similar to that reached a long while ago by pediatrics in its relation to general medicine. In pediatrics, the branching off from the parental discipline was justified by human and administrative considerations. The difficulties encountered in providing appropriate medical care for children in the adult ward or outpatient department led to a recognition of the need for separation of the two branches of medical practice. Thus pediatrics gained relative independence and could pursue research interests in its own right—research interests which moreover led to reciprocation from time to time in general medicine, as the work of Schick, Pirquet, and others has shown.

Child psychiatry too shows the first signs of a similar development, though it is still far from having outgrown its infancy. Child psychiatry has built up a method of investigation of its own—

the play technique—and has departed considerably from the method of direct questioning in favor of observing and interpreting the child's behavior. Child psychiatry, because of its intrinsic reliance on the child's family, has always regarded the child's social dependence as an essential factor in its diagnostic, therapeutic, and preventive measures. How far these facts alone have already influenced general psychiatric thinking, how strongly they have enhanced the trend toward listening to and understanding the psychiatric patient, is difficult to assess at present. Those who remember the first publications on what was called "the art of the psychotic" will also remember that attention was drawn to psychotic self-expression at a time when the pioneers of art education had just discovered the child's ability to express himself through drawing, paintings, and modelling.

Much could be said on the influence child psychiatry has had on modern ideas of general psychiatric training. Before qualifying for entry to specialist work in psychiatry, many young doctors in England undergo one year of training at a child guidance clinic, and this experience provides them with a new, significantly social and human outlook on their future work. Moreover, the need to establish from the start an emotional rather than a purely intellectual contact (with the young patient and his parents) gives the young psychiatrist a powerful impetus to acquire those human qualities which have long been cherished in successful social work.

As a result of his experiences with children the young psychiatrist is more willing and able to trace in himself his own limitations of empathy, patience and understanding of the mentally unbalanced. He is also forced to recognize and face his own psychological rigidity and prejudices. Psychiatrists who can deal successfully with these aspects of their own personalities appear to become versatile and adjustable to general psychotherapeutic work with patients of any age. From the failures they experience they become more aware of limitations which they cannot remedy by reading or more learning, and in consequence they decide to arrange personal, training, or educational analysis for themselves.

It was just this problem of the adult's difficulties in finding a workable approach to the child-patient which induced Freud, at the beginning of the century, to venture on the first psychoanalysis of the neurosis of a child (with the aid of the child's father). I refer here to the treatment of a phobia of a five-year-old boy, the well-known little Hans (1909), who was terrified by the idea of leaving his home, experiencing what amounted to a phobia of horses. While Freud kept in the background, the actual work of study and treatment was conducted by the father, a man who had a sympathetic understanding of Freud's discoveries about infantile sexuality.

It is interesting to note that this treatment by remote control then unique, has been revived recently, that is fifty years later, on a larger scale. The tremendous postwar demand for child guidance work— as child psychiatry is mostly called in Great Britain—has required a further division of labor within child guidance teams. The burden of diagnostic and administrative work necessarily shouldered by the psychiatrist in charge of a clinic largely prevented his carrying out intensive therapy. Abreactive play therapy of one or two hours a week or fortnightly has proved in many cases neither specific enough nor as effective in child therapy as interpretive methods. Moreover, this work could not be delegated to the testing psychologist nor to the psychiatric social worker, who had neither training nor time for it. Thus a strong need was felt for a new professional group: trained child therapists who could employ the techniques which have come from the experimental and research experiences of child psychoanalysis.

In England, the initiative for organizing such training came from Anna Freud, who started the Hampstead Child Therapy Course in London some years ago. Recently a model clinic has been established with the general support of the Field Foundation, and the first qualified child therapists have for some time been reinforcing the badly needed therapeutic staff at various child guidance clinics. The Child Department of the Tavistock Clinic, under the directorship of Dr. John Bowlby, has started a similar course.

Developments like these, gratifying as they are, nevertheless call for some thought about the dangers of progressive specialization and about the means of counteracting them. The young psychiatrist who specializes in child guidance will sooner or later find himself in charge of a clinic with from sixty to one-hundred-and-twenty treatment cases and sometimes a long waiting list. For him psychiatry and psychopathology will become confined to childhood, and he will lose many valuable scientific contacts which are essential for seeing the whole of development as well as its separate parts. His pediatric experience may be scanty, and yet he constantly studies and treats children in whose history bodily illness, hospitalization, and special treatment (e.g., orthopedic treatment) have played a significant part. It is a well-known fact, often regretted, that the services which modern society offers the child operate in isolation from one another, through lack of coordination and human contact. Such coordinated contact is not only beneficial for the work itself but stimulates research into fields which at present are either neglected or separated by professional barriers.

There are few topics in child psychiatry which do not bear joint implications for pediatrics, psychiatry, and problems of social organizations. Of these I should like to discuss one which provides a particularly striking example of the interdependence of these branches of knowledge—the problem of separation anxiety.

The investigation of separation of the young child from its mother has begun to have a very stimulating effect both on child psychiatry and on pediatrics. Outstanding is Dr. Rene Spitz's work, (1945,1946) especially his investigation of "anaclitic depression" in infants. The problem itself has long been known and has been investigated in the course of research on the causation of certain forms of delinquency (Bowlby, 1944), and on the effects of becoming an orphan or of being adopted. Wartime experiences in Britain, particularly the evacuation of chlidren and their placement in billets and foster homes, made interest in the subject crucial. Studies like those carried out in the Hampstead War Nurseries by Dorothy Burlingham and Anna Freud (1943, 1944) have deepened our psychological insight into the problem. Anna Freud (1951) has also studied a number of war orphans who were brought to England from German concentration camps shortly after the war. In England Dr. John Bowlby is at present conducting a thorough and widely based investigation into many problems of separation and has prepared a report on Maternal Care and Mental Health on behalf of the World Health Organization (1951). In collaboration with Bowlby, James Robertson (1953) recently produced a documentary film in which he aimed at showing the reactions of a girl of two-and-a-half to a short stay in hospital. This film is important because it provides data both on the experience of separation from the mother and on the impact of a new and strange environment upon the child. A two-and-a-half year old girl, Laura, had to undergo a minor operation for an umbilical hernia. She had not been specially chosen for the study; the surgical unit of a London hospital which cooperated in the investigation was merely asked to give the name of a young child who was just about to undergo surgery. No psychological examination was made beforehand, but a film record was taken of Laura at home just before being called to undergo the operation and then, at regular intervals and specified times, in hospital from the day of admission to that of departure. The child received the best surgical and medical attention and outstanding nursing care, and visits by the parents were arranged almost every day. Mr. Robertson had arranged a strict schedule of time sampling and thus excluded the temptation to record emotional reactions which he might have anticipated. Nevertheless the film shows the reactions which those focusing on the separation syndrome must have foreseen. We see a child deeply upset at times, sometimes withdrawn, sometimes in tears, listless, and apathetic.

The operation itself was certainly a very minor one. In her critical review of this film Anna Freud (1953), pointed out that audiences of professional nursing staff would be struck above all by the high standard of nursing and the comparative informality of the hospital atmosphere in which parents share an occasional teatime with their child and even some cherished possessions from home are admitted into the hospital bed. In spite of the admirable care for the child's well-being, psychologists will point out that the film provides evidence enough to call for a closer re-examination of current methods of hospitalization, or at least for the realization that such necessary interventions are fraught with danger for the child's emotional development.

Summarizing the sequence of emotional events during Laura's short stay in hospital, Anna Freud comments that most of the

pictures show the girl in the grip of strong emotions. At first there is
the shock of sudden separation from the mother when she is taken to
the bathroom by a most friendly nurse: panic at the realization that
her body has been delivered into the hands of an unknown person.
Terror again when she receives rectal anaesthesia and yet again
when the operation stitches are removed. The demonstration gains
added interest because the girl is of unusual intelligence, maturity,
and self-control. Under the circumstances the film might have
turned out to be a record of the emotional breakdown of a young
child: instead it gives evidence of a prolonged battle between the
child's ego forces and her affects, clearly illustrating both the child's
anxiety and her defensive activities against it. Laura often picks at
her face and pushes her hair in defense against anxiety and
subsequent crying. She projects her desire for mother when she says
"My mummy is crying for me. Go and fetch her." The battle reaches
its height when the child immobilizes her whole body in the effort to
quiet her feelings, or when her attempts not to cry are shown to lead,
by way of drying her eyes, to a complulsive rubbing which is reduced
finally to an aimless, abortive, automatic movement of the fingers
on her face. Those who expect that such emotional experiences will
be alleviated by abreactive play will not find confirmation in the
film. The time for such abreactive play has not yet come; the
emotions are still so overwhelming that they block the avenues of
discharge. The child is subjected here to a time lag similar to that
seen in the adult who cannot shed tears immediately after a severe
loss has befallen him, or perceive pain until the shock has passed
away. Whatever play activity she shows confirms the impression of a
listless child who plays in superficial attempts to please her mother
or the nurse. The toys her mother took with her to hospital fill the
role of what Donald W. Winnicott (1953) has called "the child's
transitional object." They are not just toys but links between the
lonely child and her home. Analytic experience suggests in her
relation to her toys Laura represents how she would like to be
treated—i.e., held and cuddled by her mother.

    For two days after discharge Laura was unusually anxious and
irritable. Her voice took on a high pitch, and she slept badly. She
soiled herself several times. But after two days her parents felt that

she was her pre-separation self again. Four months later her mother went to the hospital to have a second baby. Laura went to her grandmother's and did not see father or mother for five weeks. When she was reunited with them she recognized her father immediately and was friendly with him, but she failed to recognize her mother and for two days treated her politely but as a stranger. She remembered the location of things in her home but for her mother alone did not immediately show her former affection.

In discussing the entire area of children visiting or being visited in hospitals, one should mention the experimental work being carried out, at the Baby Hospital in Newcastle-on-Tyne, England, under Professor Sir James C. Spence(1947).He has found it very beneficial to both mother and infant to admit the mother to hospital with the baby and let her do all but the technical nursing. Professor Spence is also experimenting with the home care of chronically ill children, especially with those suffering from tuberculosis bone disease who would ordinarily spend years in sanatoria. All these experiments and innovations aim at assessing the role of the emotional relationship between mother and child during illness and its effect on the course of illness and during recovery.

It is now realized that an integrative effort from both sides, from pediatrics and from psychiatry, is needed to understand the psychological implications of the child's falling ill. Separation from the mother owing to hospitalization is but one of a wider set of crises including the effect of surgery preformed on the child, the effect of anaesthesia, and various psychosomatic problems. These issues have been widely discussed, but what is not fully realized is the present division among the workers concerned; there is a group of pediatricians, nurses, and hospital staff who are closely acquainted only with the physically ill child; there is another group, the teachers, child psychiatrists, and child therapists who know only the physically healthy child. Yet when the child receives medical care, he is still the same child who yesterday attended school or was treated for some behavior disorder, neurosis or even some psychosomatic complaint. Workers in the field of child psychiatry and child guidance have little direct knowledge of their patient's reactions and actual behavior in states of bodily illness. Contact with the child almost always ceases, yet psychoanalytic work with children proves that experiences of pain, fever, minor surgery, or even a medical examination immediately engage the child's emotions and fantasy life. It is only the mothers, who have an opportunity to see their children in health, illness, and convalescence, who can tell us how they deviate from the norm, bodily and mentally, and how they return to their former selves. On the other hand, during severe bodily illness or even at the suspicion of severe illness, the mother's concentration on nursing activities and her emotional involvement act to distort her judgment and leave little room for objective observation of the child's psychological reaction to illness.

In London, Anna Freud (1952) has for a long time been collecting observations from many intimate contacts with children under analysis, and has recently reviewed the problem of the role of bodily illness in the mental life of children. Whereby she has also succeeded in putting the problem of separation anxiety due to hospitalization in better perspective.

From her work and from general observation we know that every bodily illness makes an additional demand on man's adaptive resources, as it does on the adaptive resources of his environment. The child's first notion that his body is falling ill may therefore depend on his mother's reactions to the initial signs. If a mother's attitude is rather ascetic and aims at minimizing the importance of illness, the child may be induced to deny in himself the need for more warmth, both literally and figuratively, and so his illness may pass unnoticed, or he may succumb only after psychological resistances have broken down. In other cases the denying of additional care for the sick body will cause the child to react to an illness as if it were a hostile intrusion, exposing him to unwanted frustrations which can be dealt with only by turning to depression, apathy, or deep sleep.

When, however, in consequence of an illness, the emotional climate becomes much warmer, the child may find himself in a position of comparatively unlimited fulfillment of desires, such as being in sole possession of his mother or having his body handled by her once more. Surprisingly, in spite of their pleasantness, these nursing procedures may become a source of bewilderment and minor upheaval. When the demands to observe toilet training and eating habits are relaxed, pleasant as that may be for the child, it may also have the meaning of a regression, of being forced back into a secretly desired state, and revolt of the conscious personality against such regression may ensue. For the child it may assume the meaning of having successfully rivalled a younger sibling, and thus guilt may be aroused. Because of the pleasant emotions it experiences in the nursing situation, the child may feel as if it had indulged in pleasure which its ideals and self-esteem oppose, or it may feel seduced to regress in its behavior and may find it difficult to progress after recovery. The psychological situation is comparable to that of a student who, tempted by his colleagues, gets drunk and reacts either with self-contempt or with the wish to have the experience repeated all over again.

In contrast to the enforced regression to earlier levels of instinct gratification, in its motor activities the sick child, especially under conditions of home nursing, generally does not easily accept restrictions of movement. When such restrictions have to be enforced and amount to restraint, the commonly known sequelae of orthopedic treatment enter the picture. Their bearing on the development of aggression and of tic-like movements has been noted, as has the compensatory acceleration of ego skills, especially of speech development. Anna Freud reports that a girl, immobilized in the course of orthopedic treatment, used to pay her friends out of her pocket money for every new swear word they brought home from school. The use of bad language was the only outlet for otherwise paralyzed activity and aggression.

There is one aspect of the nursing procedure with which psychoanalysts are very well acquainted but which is difficult to convey without arousing strong disbelief and the suspicion that it is an exceptional reaction. In their rather autistic and animistic way of thinking, children sometimes interpret the administration of medicine as the giving of poison. They thus admit to consciousness, in the form of a suspicion or accusation, that which is part of an unconscious relationship to their mothers, a relationship tinged by aggression and fears of retaliation. So far only through the psychoanalytic treatment of small children has it been possible to elucidate such fantasies in *statu nascendi* and deal with them on the spot. Their psychiatric significance cannot be overestimated.

Turning now to the child's psychological response to surgical and dental interventions, one naturally hesitates to touch on a subject which has been discussed thoroughly and expertly in the United States.

For psychoanalysts the possible psychological effect of surgery on childhood development is a question of long standing. Any surgical intervention, even the mere idea of it or knowledge of it from hearsay, merges with man's fantasy of being exposed to pain and mutilation. The fantasy springs from his need to be loved and the fear of deprivation of such security, and also from his feelings of guilt and expectation of retaliation. It is an essential part of psychoanalytic experience that these fantasies and fears are rooted in the oral-aggressive and anal-sadistic phases of emotional development and culminate in the child's oedipal phase with its castration complex and fantasy. The impact of the knowledge or actual experience of surgery is therefore secondary to the anticipatory anxieties and fantasies. These themselves are ubiquitous and arise independently of actual threats from outside. This happsens when the struggle between the instinctual drives of sadistic and phallic qualities and the drive opposing and restricting ego activities is at its height. Considerations of avoidance of the castration effect which so much concerned the pioneers in the field of psychiatric prevention in the past are now considered outdated. The focal point for the assessment of the psychological effect of surgery on the child is therefore the fantasy life of the average child: the impact of the actual threat of punishment in the form of surgery can only be understood as it interacts with the perception of threat and punishment in these fantasies. Therefore it has to be underlined again that the meaning of an operation for a child or for an apprehensive adult is highly overdetermined.

Much room remains for experimentation on how best to prepare the child psychologically for a surgical or dental operation and on the measures to be taken during and after such intervention to alleviate the potential trauma. Anna Freud suggests that, in deciding on the length of the preparation time before an operation, we take two factors into account: a preparation period that is too lengthy leaves too much time for the child's reaction in fantasies. The anticipatory stress excites fantasies which the child conceives according to his developmental level and not according to the actual operation. Where the interval between knowledge of an impending operation and its actual performance is too short, the ego has insufficient time to prepare and summon its defenses. This consideration applies to all emergency operations.

In speaking of the child's fantasies, one perhaps conveys a wrong idea of actual imagery, of fantasy pictures or daydreams, in which the operation itself or its imagined results are elaborated in an unrealistic morbid fashion. But this in fact is not what we have in mind when, as psychoanalysts, we speak of the imagination of the child or of the hysterical or psychotic patient. These fantasies can take the form of anything from a vauge feeling of threat to a full elaboration of how threat will affect the body. The imagined threat may range from lasting separation from the mother to total mutilation of the body, from the feeling of being maltreated to that of being turned into something like an animal or monster. Again it may take the form of being punished and of suffering retaliation for feelings of hate and aggression or cruelty—emotions which the child himself may have felt toward others, of which he has made drawings or about which he has dreamed. Such images usually have a more dreamlike character than do actual visual pictures, and their effect may be similar to that of a dream turning into a nightmare. According to his individual state of development, the child may imagine that to be operated upon means to be handled like an animal, taken to be slaughtered, handled like a carcass, like excrement, or tossed about live leaves in the wind (Melanie Klein, 1948). For a small child surgery may assume the meaning of what he does to his doll or toy animal, when he tears it open and empties it of its contents. Of course, the normal secure child has many motives for not turning toward such notions and for not letting them get a hold in his conscious fantasy. The normal child will turn away from them in horror. When they appear in sleep and dreams, the child protects himself by waking up and calling for the protecting mother. He can succeed in laughing them away and, by achieving this, he reassures himself as the mother does, and denies the feeling of anxiety attached to the idea of danger—in relation both to the actual operation and to the anaesthesia.

Denial is linked with repression and thus it fosters unrest during sleep, nightmares or depressing dreams, since repressions do not work reliably during sleep. Children who laugh away the fact that one sometimes has to face painful experiences develop an unrealistic need to appear courageous. They may expose themselves to injury and accidents because they have become psychologically blind to danger. Others, by successfully repressing emotions of anxiety or panic, cling to their mothers, behave very reasonably and well on the surface and tolerate everything done to them. They may adopt as a protective attitude a rather tolerant, perhaps even masochistic relationship towards other people, accept discomfort and pain without reacting, and thus in later life may provoke others, the more aggressive ones, to make use of their tolerance to their own detriment.

But if the ego has enough time to prepare for shock—not too much and not too little—it can build up its normal defenses. First, the child will identify with the mother's confidence and, while he will be aware of anxieties, he will not feel alone with them; he will have a feeling that the mother is somewhat anxious too, but confident as well. He will react with curiosity, the precondition for increasing knowledge and foresight. When the actual pain and shock have passed, abreactive play will help to turn the passively experienced trauma into playful activity. The integration of experiences during illness and hospitalization will be expected to extend over a much longer period than the bodily healing process itself—and those psychological scars which will always remain may or may not have future significance.

The child's overt reactions to anxiety and pain, to the increase of attention and comfort he may receive during an illness and the temptations and threats he may experience during the nursing activities, do not cover the whole picture the psychologist feels compelled to study when considering the ill child. One thinks of the poet's description of his toothache: "Concentrated is the soul in his jaw tooth's aching hole" (Freud, 1914). It is this *concentration of inner interest,* this shift of the hypothetical mental energy toward the disturbance of inner equilibrium, to which we should now turn.

The ill body shows a heightened demand for libidinal cathexis. In some children this demand makes itself felt by a sudden onrush of symptoms. Judged by their behavior, their lassitude, sudden failure of appetite and usual interests, they appear more ill than one would expect from the temperature or the nature of the illness. Mothers who know their chlidren well can spot an oncoming indisposition or disease from such behavioral reactions.

There are both withdrawing and demanding types of ill children. Withdrawal from the object world is associated with a lack of contact with and interest in the surroundings. Children reacting in this way do not make strong appeals to their mothers to be helped or relieved from discomfort or pain. They have more or less cut their communication lines with the environment; they may lack their normal affectionate contact, even appear strange to their mothers, who complain about lack of affection and demand on them; some mothers, inclined to react with guilt, take the child's withdrawal as a personal rejection and accusation. It would be helpful to know whether these children behaved in a similar way in infancy, whether they were crying infants or more silent ones, and if so what their earliest attitudes to infant feeding were, or when they woke up from sleep, what their attitudes had been to light, sounds, and stimulation in general. In illness they always give the impression of being seriously ill, yet they expend the minimum amount of energy, and do not move about much until the illness subsides. These children give no indication of resentment against the mother for their having fallen ill. We shall have to think of this type again when we consider hypochondriacal reactions to illness.

The second group does not show narcissistic, protective withdrawal but makes demands upon the mother. In contrast to the former group of children, they do not want to be left alone, they regress in their social behavior, may become more babyish, refuse to read in bed and prefer to look at pictures or make drawings, their skill in drawing being definitely regressed. They are inclined to complain and generally behave as if something had gone wrong, not in their body, but in their surroundings. They are easily kept in bed and enjoy being, nay, demand to be, nursed. While the former type easily falls asleep whether the mother is near or the light on or not, this type demands, rather, to have the mother at the bedside when going to sleep and the light dim but not completely turned off.

Some children when ill take active charge of their bodies for the duration of the illness. They not only cooperate willingly with the mother, the nurse or the doctor, but observe meticulously whatever the doctor has ordered to be done. They watch the clock so that they get the medicine strictly at the prescribed time; if not intimidated they ask questions and try to draw attention to what they momentarily think is in need of explanation.

Looking at the various shades of behavior of the sick child from the surface, we might conclude that any given reaction is the normal reaction of the child to a new experience, and we would note his ability to identify with the adult and take over in a childish way what he believes to be essential. However, psychoanalytic experience with children just recovered from an illness offers different explanations. Often the child's activity or overactivity during illness turns out to be his inner response to a suspicion of being neglected or of not fully trusting the mother, who could not prevent her child's becoming ill. Another explanation put forward by those having intimate contact with children is still more complicated, or, as some may be inclined to think, sophisticated. We believe that some chilren, when ill or after having hurt themselves, identify themselves with their mother and treat the ill part of their body, or what they feel is the illness, as if it were they themselves—the child or even the child as a baby. For many children and adults, symptoms are felt as either something strange and new whose presence is to be denied, to be shaken off, or to be taken very seriously, observed, watched and looked for in other parts of the body. The symptoms become personified, the body feels as if it had been invaded by something strange and upsetting from outside. One thinks of medieval illustrations of diseased organs, invaded by strange animals or parasites. The strange, new feeling in the body stimulates autisitc, unrealistic thinking and partly explains the withdrawal reaction of the ill person.

Observations suggesting some support for this view were made at the Hampstead War Nurseries (Burlingham and Anna Freud, 1944) on children who were either permanently or temporarily separated from their mothers. Some children showed an excessive concern about their physical health and, when ill, about their sick body, despite the absence of a worrying mother. They seemed not to enjoy their state of freedom from overprotective mothers but took over their role of their own accord. They insisted, quite contrary to expectation, on wearing protective clothes, rubber boots, overcoats etc., even when encouraged not to do so unnecessarily: one or the other even recorded their times of sleep and in general perpetuated the motherly care of which they were actually deprived. An instructive example referred to is a motherless boy of six, who, in a long drawn-out night of vomiting and diarrhoea, was heard to say to himself "I, my darling." When asked what he meant, he answered "That I love myself. It is good to love oneself, isn't it?"

We thus come to the conclusion that some children's relationships to their own bodies resemble that of the adult hypochondriac. They treat their bodies, or parts of them, as if they had lost their mothers' loving care and attention and now have to do it themselves. It is noteworthy that the hypochondriacal phase which frequently precedes a psychotic episode was explained long ago in a similar way. The changes in the patient's perceptions of his environment, the threating loss of contact with other people, the feeling of strangeness toward the beloved ones, is responded to by an increasing attention to the body, or parts of it, which—as has often been shown—once played an important role in the development of his relationship to objects he loved.

To summarize briefly:

1) Child psychiatry plays an important part in the training of the future psychiatrist. Learning how to make contact with child psychiatric cases and the acquisition of special psychological techniques of treatment are now considered useful pre-requisites for the psychotherapeutic handling of adult psychotics and borderline cases in general psychiatric practice. In his personal contact with children, the psychiatrist more easily recognizes his own emotional rigidity and the fixed patterns of his responses.

2) In addressing an area in which child psychiatry and pediatrics overlap, we have looked at the child's reaction to hospitalization in

order to learn more about his reaction to separation from the mother and the family in general. It can be said that the child's sadness when separated from the mother is an appropriate response to his own feelings of loneliness and deprivation. Psychopathological considerations suggest that expression of this reponse should be fostered rather than ignored or suppressed, if hospitalization combined with separation from the mother is unavoidable.

3) From the study of the effect of bodily illness on the child two general conclusions can be drawn:

(a) Illness affects the child's emotional relationship to his environment. It may lead to a regressive clinging to the mother or to a reproachful or helpless and hopeless turning away from her. Both tendencies have an important bearing on the development of psychopathological traits among which manifest or latent anxiety states are the earliest ones; symptom neuroses, like nightmares, bed-wetting and tics and later sequelae.

(b) Bodily illness can lead to a withdrawal of attachment to the object world and result in a concentration on the body or part of it. The child can thus develop hypochondria-like attitudes to himself or come to consider the environment as hostile, unloving, and in general dangerous.

7

Infant Observations and Concepts Relating to Infancy

(THE FREUD ANNIVERSARY LECTURE)*

For the third time in the history of the Freud Anniversary Lectures, your choice of lecturer has fallen upon a psychoanalyst from outside the United States. Like my predecessors on the other two occasions, I have neither grown nor matured in this fertile soil and in this climate which, like none other, have proved so well suited to the promotion of Freud's work. Can it be true, I ask, that from now on I may pride myself on being one of your Freud Anniversary lecturers and that, as one from the Old World, I now enter into a new association with Anna Freud and Ernest Jones?

Whatever this honor may mean to me and to some of my colleagues here and abroad, the fact remains that it is due to your generous recognition of a service I have been trying to render to psychoanalysis over the past forty years. I cannot delude myself and consider this honor as raising me to the status of a member of the elite, for no such thing exists—in my opinion—except in man's illusion.

The theme I am about to develop cannot have come as a surprise when you first heard of the title of this lecture. Nevertheless, you must have been wondering just what I should venture to contribute to the rich body of new observations, explanatory comments and theories, which American psychoanalysis has already added to the revolutionary basic teaching of Freud on the dawn of mind. Your own workers have elaborated on Freud's original thinking. They have—so to speak—modernized Freud's observations and conceptions of infancy and childhood and have fundamentally influenced our knowledge and thinking on "what infancy is about."

This is the point at which one might naturally recall the galaxy of names, discoveries and brilliant ideas, which stand for the psychoanalytic study of infancy and childhood in America. Today I single out for mention here just two of your workers, Edith Jacobson for her book *The Self and the Object World* (1965) and Rene Spitz for his recent *The First Year of Life* (1965).

New observations and changes in theory do call from time to time for new attempts at integration and for necessary adjustments and corrections of previously held tenets. Still, your sense of responsibility has proved highly alert not only to the tasks but also to the dangers of this post-Freudian age. You have given, and will give, serious thought to the question why some observations and theoretical innovations ought merely to be noted, whereas others can be accepted and become part of the Freudian tradition.

Thanks to James Strachey and to the support of his venture by American psychoanalysis, from now on the English reader too can familiarize himself fully with Freud's own writings. Using these as a yardstick in our evaluations, are we not all concerned lest we dig graves and bury, together with the outdated and obsolete, those valuables which were better protected and preserved, not for eternity but for a forseeable future?

Thoughts and considerations like these were quite painfully on one's mind some twenty years ago, when storms of disputation were raging in the British Psycho-Analytical Society. You have become familiar with Melanie Klein's "expansion" of Freudian theory and have shown interest in her bold changes of technique and in her teaching about the infant's psyche. Her aspirations however, or— more strictly speaking, those of her more ardent supporters— tended less to be an enrichment than a substitute for the mainstream of Freudian thinking.

In addition to the controversy with Melanie Klein, I found myself facing a challenge which forced me to an immediate reaction, which had to be reasoned and not dogmatic. Luckily I learned to share this reaction with some of my British colleagues, particularly with Marjorie Brierley and Edward Glover; I should like to call it "a near scientific reaction." As a teacher of the traditional or classical thinking of Freud about the mind and its development, and particularly its psychosexual aspects, I found myself confronted by a majority of students who had learned to stand up for their own ideas, not only with some passion—this was hoped for and welcomed—but with arguments which could not be discarded as outside the scope of scientific discourse.

Had the disputation just been about Melanie Klein's inferences, which she brought to bear on her audience's mind through the strength of her personality and her rigid convictions, its outcome would have been, in my opinion, only a question of time. Her teaching, based as it was after 1932 on too concrete a rendering of Freud's Eros-Thanatos hypothesis, would have melted away in the sun of scientific development and scrutiny, together with her optimistic, but now widely discredited, superior therapeutic claims. But there was more to be found in the student's arguments and criticism of the Freudian tradition and that at a time when ego psychology was still in the making.

An integral part of the teaching the London student of psychoanalysis received at that time was the work of Karl Abraham (1927) on the vicissitudes of the instinctual drives, e.g., the oral-biting phase of the infant. There was also Sandor Ferenczi's teaching—not his "active," technique, which London had rejected, but his impressive claims about the importance of the otherwise well-known interaction between the infant's internal conflicts and the mother's response to them (1926). In 1937 Andre Peto tried to substantiate such a claim through observations of the neonate-mother feeding relationship.

In spite of the impression their personalities had made on me as a newcomer during the 1920s, I had not given the thinking of Karl Abraham and Sandor Ferenczi the full attention they deserved. By that I mean that I had underrated the role of aggression and object-directed hostility in human life, infancy included. This led me to take more seriously the truth in Freud's own teaching, namely that the science of mental processes, functioning, and organization—in other words, everything that refers to brain functioning—must not be tied too closely to the behavioral evidence it can provide.

Anticipating a later part of this lecture, I should like to mention an idea on mental functioning to which I feel committed. I have referred to the infant's early conflicts and the mother's response to them. I believe it is more than mere speculation to think of some conflicting mental processes being active when we speak of the infant's need and the need-satisfying object and of the regulatory function of the pleasure-pain principle. I think there is "conflict in suspense" (whatever this may mean) in the dreamy infant of whom Edith Jacobson speaks and "conflict solution" when wakefulness changes into sleep and vice versa. Phyllis Greenacre's "The Biological Economy of Birth" (1945) not only strongly reinforced this position but was instrumental in my coming to such a belief.

In addition to my neglect of Abraham and Ferenczi, I found myself lacking an integrated knowledge of the finer points of the psychological teaching of Freud himself. I began to enjoy anew, among many others, the paper "On Negation" (1925) and "The Uncanny" (1919). To be more blunt, I had to move from the more comfortable and clinically appropriate ground of psychoanalytic behaviorism to the slippery and hazardous ground of pure psychoanalytic psychology. Here one had to commit oneself to inferences fraught wth the danger of becoming more and more anthropomorphic or adult-omorphic, an expression the late John B. Benjamin used when he referred to Melanie Klein's propositions about early infancy. I do not believe, however, that one necessarily becomes a Kleinian as a result of probing into infancy.

To make an excursion into the early stages of oral psychology, as Bertram Lewin aptly called it in 1945, would have been impossible without the facilities provided and opportunities offered by Dorothy Burlingham and Anna Freud in the Hampstead War Nurseries during the years 1940 to 1946. I refer here to my tenty-minute contribution to the first post-war conference of European Psychoanalysts at Amsterdam (1947) "Mouth, Hand and Ego Integration."

The aim of the paper was twofold. To my knowledge no direct observations, such as my own, had previously been reported which, even if only tentatively, could substantiate for the first half year of life two pertinent statements in Freud's *The Ego and the Id* (1923), namely that the ego is a product of differentiation from the id and that the ego is first and foremost a body-ego.

I could have bypassed the two Freudian hypotheses and brought my observations directly into line with the still very recent new propositions by Hartmann, Kris, and Loewenstein in "Comments on the Formation of Psychic Structure" (1946). My observations accorded with their views. Had I done so, I would have suggested that the "undifferentiated state of mental organization" turns into "differentiation of the Id and Ego" at a definite age which—for the infants observed—was the third and fourth months of life. Hartmann, Kris, and Loewenstein had explicitly "refrained from indicating at what time during early infancy the successive steps leading to structural differentiation take place." And in any event I would not now advocate any definite or rigid fixing of developmental timetables, for reasons which I shall discuss later when speaking of the part customs in infant-rearing play in addition to the pre-patterned evolution of the id and ego.

The second aim of my paper was to indicate that the mouth-hand relationship, following the psychological birth-trauma period, brings about a differentiation of self-sensations and object sensations, the pathfinders for self-representation and object representation. By this I mean that the feeding experiences of infants aged twelve to sixteen weeks and brought up under somewhat special but in no way exceptional circumstances, created sensations of object quality which contrasted with the double-simultaneous sensations elicited by the infant himself on his own body, for instance by way of mouth-finger contact and the kinesthetic sensations belonging to it. I was compelled to infer that infants of that age had to be accorded a differentiating and discriminating faculty of this kind. It was only after many viewings of the film which depicted these activities, that it dawned on me—against inner resistances—that these activities *already* exhibited the general functional characteristics of the ego which Freud had outlined in *The Ego and the Id* (1923). In 1950 I was privileged to read a paper on "Development of the Body-Ego" at a symposium of the Aerican Psychoanalytic Association on "Psychoanalysis and Developmental Psychology." I feel indebted to Louis Linn, who, in 1955, tried to correlate these observations to neurological data provided mainly by Morris B. Bender in 1952.

Otto Isakower's classical paper on the "Patho-Psychology of Phenomena associated with Falling Asleep" (1938) contains more information on infant psychology than the author attempted to enlarge upon by way of extrapolation and inference. It is well toward the closing pages of this paper that Isakower suggests, with all the caution characteristic of that time, that one might take "the hypothesis seriously—namely, that we have here a revivial of very early ego-attitudes." Further, he asks whether the reproductions in the phenomenon now called after him "do not perhaps bear the imprint of external stimulations with which these [ego-] attitudes were contemporaneous." Isakower adds, "I am well aware of the conjectural nature of the answer I am inclined to make. Yes, these imprints seem very easy to detect; they are mental images of sucking at the mother's breast and of falling asleep there when satisfied."

What was then necessarily emphasized as being conjectural—like the dream screen—we now accept as contents of the infant's unconscious. You will see presently that psychoanalysts can differ remarkably in their opinion as to whether or not these unconscious representations carry object-qualities. The "crumbled or sandy feeling in the mouth," a detail in the Isakower phenomenon, provides an example of such differences in evaluation. Isakower expressed the view that the sandy feeling in the mouth of the dreamer points to "the unpleasant and unfamiliar," for the intra-uterine state probably never included anything of that sort.

The genetic derivation of dryness in the mouth, which Isakower suggests, was fully concordant with our thinking and preconceptions at that time. One can assume in retrospect that hardly anybody would have argued differently then. Now, however, one may ask why no one thought about the infant's salivary glands dealing with any dryness in the mouth, or am I wrong, do they not function so early? Before I suggest a different explanation of the dreamer's sensations, I must mention Rene A. Spitz's evaluation (1944). He finally comes to the conclusion that the sandy sensations in the dreamer's mouth are non-representational.

My own viewpoint leads me even beyond Isakower's. Disregarding his wise caution, I conjecture along the following lines: I ask why the reproduction of a sandy, gritty feeling in the mouth should not have come from sensations of dryness or hardness of an object in the suckling's mouth? Why should it not have been caused by an erect, hard nipple and/or its areola? Montgomery's tubercles have been mentioned as the most likely source of such hardness and dryness. Such conditions of the nipple are not ubiquitous, but neither is the Isakower phenomenon and the sandy feeling connected with it. Perhaps one day someone will, or will not, be able to establish a correlation?

Must we not be inclined tacitly to accept a kind of negative anthropomorphism in our thinking, which sometimes counteracts our searching into causality? Can there be a negative anthropomorphism which sets limits to our imagination, expectation, cognition, observation, and reconstructive endeavor?

I have already expressed respect and admiration for the organized and systematic research work of present-day psychoanalysts. I am somewhat familiar with this pioneering work and with the results already achieved by it. Furthermore, as shown in a recent report on "Contributions of Longitudinal Studies to Psychoanalytic Theory"

(Shafer, 1965) presented to the American Psychoanalytic Association, the new methods of observation, of recording data and of
working them through must bring about new, perhaps
revolutionary results for a long time to come. Yet how much we
could still learn from oldfashioned modes of observation. The
psychoanalyst's office (consulting room) has always been one of the
most rewarding observation posts.

But now, returning to my main topic, I have to draw attention to
another observation concerning an infant, younger even than twelve
weeks, and his mouth movements. No doubt we shall all consider
these movements to have been prepatterned; nevertheless I assume
that they were loaded with mental content, however limited, taken
from the world of sensations, experiences, and expectations of his
age, namely four weeks. I cannot exclude the remote possibility that
the maturational age of that infant was nearer to eight weeks, but I
have no indication whatsoever for that, nor would it affect the issue.
In any event I am prepared to be criticized either for relying too
much on your credulity or for arguing the obvious. The observation
refers tentatively to Freud's hallucinatory wish-fulfillment which, he
said, the infant employs when bridging the time-lag between the
emergence of a need or wish and its fulfillment, entering, when it
fails, into a state of frustration, mental pain, and crying. (I shall not
argue again in favour of Freud's "negative hallucination" which, in
my opinion, precedes any response to a need or wish and thus
precedes "hallucinatory wish-fulfillment," perhaps by using
"primary identification."

To return to the case, during the closing phase of the Hampstead
War Nurseries I was informed by Sophie Dann, who was in charge
of the Baby's room, of a new arrival who showed "funny mouth
movements" just before feeding time. For the past two or three days,
the baby had been found to rouse from sleep about ten minutes
before feeding time. As usual, Miss Dann warned me to come
quickly, because some infant behavior is so transient that it comes
and goes before one can record it. I filmed the baby once, in haste. It
was several years before it dawned on me that its mouth behavior
could illustrate Freud's hallucinatory wish-fulfillment, provided
such a thing does really happen in infancy. The infant in question

woke with his mouth fully relaxed. Then the lips became somewhat restless as if a slow wave were moving over them; perhaps it was a kind of licking and perhaps more went on within the oral cavity which one could not see. Then the mouth opening became smaller, and in a second or third wave it became round, contracting into a button-hole opening which left—so I thought—just room for the nipple or teat. Soon afterward the mouth again relaxed and the bottle had to be given. That is the observation, and the film record of it still exists. Because, to my knowledge, there have been no previous reports of such an observation, I made enquiries of Dr. Sylvia Brody. She, I understand, has so far not become aware of such behavior but will look out for it.

If there is any truth in my suggestion that we had here an "hallucinatory wish-fulfillment," the objectless state of infancy can no longer be considered to be continuous for any great span of time. The absolutely objectless state has to be considered as being interrupted by fantasies of object-quality.

But had we not better reserve Freud's hallucinatory wish-fulfillment for a more developed infant? Should we not leave it to our contemporary research workers, for instance Max Schur or Peter Wolf, to explain such movements? While I willingly admit to being an adventurer in this field, as well as to the singularity of the obsevation, and further to the problem of that infant's maturation, I do not think that these authors should be considered antagonistic to such an assumption. If Max Schur—to quote Charles Fisher (1965)—"indicates that we cannot speak of instinctual drives until psychic structure develops, until the formation of the 'wish,' that is when memory traces of experienced gratification and frustration are laid down," then I do not expect him to be unwilling to accord a hearing and the status of a probability, to the casual evidence I have provided. More I cannot wish for because in that way purely psychological reasoning would have overruled extreme physio-biological and the behavioristic argumentation. One would merely grant that the "neonate state characterized by a diffuse dispersion of undifferentiated physiological energy," as emphasized by Edith Jacobson, was, in this case, of shorter duration than convention has assumed.

I do not know anything about infants' dreams, but in view of

Charles Fisher's statement (1965) on the conditions of dreaming in
infancy, I cannot expect him to deny that some evidence exists for
hallucinatory wish-fulfillment. Still less ought a rejection of
probability to be expected from Peter Wolf, unless he insists that we
must look upon the mouth movements described and, so far as I am
aware, observed only just before feeding time, as motor patterns
which have no claim to being age-appropriate indications of mental
representations for that particular infant. I do not think that Peter
Wolf will make such a claim, for he himself has given around four
weeks as the age when the discharge patterns subside in some cases
and hallucinatory wish-fulfillment can take place.

The time has not yet come for a unified theory of mental
functioning and development during infancy. This lack is due, at
least in part, to reasons Hartmann had in mind when he spoke of the
conceptual difficulties in fitting narcissism into the framework of
structural theory. So far it has not been possible to pair or match this
concept with its counterpart representing the aggressive-destructive
drive energies. A signpost to a more satisfactory solution may,
however, be seen in Edith Jacobson's book (1965).

In recent years Freud's developmental timetable of infancy and
early childhood has come under serious review, and attempts at
revising it have been made. I refer to the timetable of development
from autoerotism to absolute primary narcissism, to object cathexis
and its reconversion into secondary narcissism. Freud himself did
not always adhere to it, but neither did he explicitly revise it; he just
provided stepping-stones some of which have stood the test of time
well.

The concept of absolute primary narcissism was discussed and its
revision advocated, by the Baltimore team in 1959 (Bing, et al.). In
agreement with Edith Jacobson (1954), Bing, McLaughlin and
Marburg consider primary narcissism to be *predominantly* a
physiological state. It seems, therefore, that they do not altogether
exclude the idea of some psychic processes operating in the absolute
primary narcissistic state. The authors have come to the
conclusion—and their arguments carry considerable weight—that,
as a result of developments in ego psychology, the distinction
between primary and secondary narcissism, that is, between

primary and secondary libidinal cathexis of the psychological self, has by now lost much of its meaning.

Moreover, the authors have also come to the conclusion that the concept of "autoerotism" is in need of revision. In their opinion autoerotism refers to the cathexis of some part of the body and is not a developmental state or phase as it was assumed to be in Freud's earlier writings. Their argument pertains to that aspect of autoerotism which Humberto Nagera (1964) called "first type autoerotism." Be that as it may, autoerotism is a useful descriptive term. But one will have to be careful and consider it to be a discharge activity; it does not reveal anything of the concomitant pleasurable fantasy activity. It is noteworthy that the illustrations in Lindner's study of "sensual sucking" (1879), which was instrumental in Freud's thinking on autoerotism, show children, engaged in sensual sucking, all beyond the age of infancy and most of them between the ages of four and sixteen years. Did these children really engage in purely autoerotic pleasure, without any fantasies or daydreams? Do not some of these illustrations suggest masturbation equivalents, concomitant with unconscious fantasies?

I also discussed the problem of primary narcissism in 1959 in a paper read before the British Psycho-Analytical Society, before the publication of the Baltimore team was known to me. I felt that I could fully agree with Phyllis Greenacre (1952) who said that Freud conceived of primary narcissistic libido—a quality or type of libido, not a state—as being coincident with life; that it can be found wherever there is a spark of life; and that he attributed primary narcissism to the fetus when he said "the foetus can be aware of nothing but a gross disturbance in the economy of its narcissistic libido."

But there is also the problem of narcissism in deep, dreamless sleep, of which Freud (1917) said that "the psychical state of a sleeping person is characterized by an *almost* [my italics] complete withdrawal from the surrounding world and of all interest in it." Since Freud made this statement in the prestructural era it does not take into account the aggressive-destructive energies. It is compatible with Charles Fisher's recent statement (1965) that "mental activity goes on in all stages of sleep, the mind never rests." A proviso for such activities was made by Freud when he added "primary identification" to our conceptual armamentarium. This I understood to be operating with an amount of "mobile energy" within the primary narcissistic organization of psychic energy in the state of deep sleep. In other words, primary identification can be viewed as the functional aspect of primary narcissism. In this case it would be the first line of protection of the primary narcissistic organization; the second line, the psychic pain barrier (Hoffer, 1950, 1955), is derived from the functioning of those structures of the nervous system that subserve the pleasure-pain requirements of the organism (Robert Heath, 1964). Here we have arrived at a point which is beyond the scope of an inquiry into infancy as such though the problem of aggressive and destructive forces is also one of infancy. Edith Jacobson highlighted this point in writing about masochism (1965).

There still remains one question which can be asked about Freud's infant observation and the emergence of concepts relating to infancy. What was it that motivated Freud when he set up his timetable of the ontogenetic evolution of the mind? Why, in fact, did he speak of autoerotism, primary narcissism, object cathexis, and secondary narcissism?

In 1959, I wrote a paper "A Reconsideration of Freud's Concept 'Primary Narcissism'" (read to the British Psycho-Analytic Society but never published). Freud considered primary narcissism the original libidinal cathexis of the ego, later extended to objects. I began by asking how it had come about that the Budapest School, which certainly influenced object-relation theory, intrasigently insisted on replacing Freud's primary narcissism with the idea of primary object-love. I suggested that one of numerous answers could probably be inferred from Ernest Jones's biography of Freud (1957) and particularly from the Ferenczi-Freud relationship.

But there may be yet another explanation. I stress *may be* because I am going to put it forward simply as a suggestion, though I feel it warrants serious consideration. I would say that there is no basis for invalidating Freud's time-table of development in infancy *if* it is considered within the content of the customs and the field of observation which existed when it was drawn up. Conversely, I would say that a change in assessment of the early stages may have been occasioned—possibly misleadingly so—by a change in the field of observation. In other words, the infants Freud saw were different in some respects from the infants we see today. It may be worth considering these differences to see whether it is due to them, rather than to a reassessment of the basic similarities, that changes of concepts have been made.

My thoughts on the differences in the field of observation rest largely upon the fact and effects of that form of infant rearing known as swaddling. There is quite a considerable literature on swaddling and on the effect of motor restraint in infant rearing. Ruth Benedict (1949) wrote about it, but her observations, like those of Gorer and Rickman (1949) and of Erik Erikson on Gorki (1950) were made in cultures which were not only somewhat different from, but also less developed than the one of interest in this context. The effects of deprivation and restraint have been investigated by Phyllis Greenacre (1944) and more recently commented on by Sylvia Brody (1956). Siegfried Bernfeld's *The Psychology of the Infant* (1929) can still be considered an ancient monument of psychoanalytic interest in infancy but his enquiry was not based on direct observations made by himself. Bernfeld called swaddling the fetus-philic custom, in contrast to the fetus-phobic custom, which follows the Spartan way of infant rearing; Margaret Mead has shown a film in which this latter custom is illustrated by an almost complete absence of bodily contact between the mother and the naked child; the feeding mother leans over the child while it is lying of a leaf or on the bare soil. Also of note is a supplement to *Pediatrics* on swaddling and experimental observations, published in 1965 by an American team of pediatricians. The preliminary result of this investigation seems to indicate that swaddling definitely decreases physiological activity and frequency of response and that the swaddled infant sleeps more than the unswaddled but—this may be reassuring to some of us— that the swaddled infant still continues to interact with the environment; that is, that swaddling does not necessarily make the infant dull.

Let us now consider the infants Freud himself observed. I assumed in 1959, and have no reason to change this view, that the infants Freud saw as a medical student and doctor, but especially as the father of six children, were swaddled infants. This has been confirmed by at least one of the six (Mrs. Mathilde Hollitscher). It must be remembered that swaddling in some form was still quite customary in the culture in which Freud made his observations and had his personal experience with infants and children. Let us assume that these were moderately swaddled infants, they were nonetheless restrained to a degree which, except when they were being cleaned, left little freedom for expression, save facial expression. From the beginning of this century onward I myself have seen many infants being fed in their swaddling clothes and am certainly not the only such witness present at this lecture. I imagine that when Freud saw infants in his medical career they were freed from their swaddling, gear for medical inspection and examination.

I have referred to the existing studies of swaddling and its effects, and no psychoanalyst will suggest that swaddling will not leave its mark on the mind. But this mark need not be a pathological one, and the swaddled infant certainly survives. One of them has the honor of addressing you today!

Slightly modifying an expression once used by Sandor Rado we might say that swaddling clothes and bands provide the infant with a narcissistic rind or shell which surrounds his developing body-ego. They enclose the infant, thereby not only restraining it from movement but also shielding it, shutting it off from many stimuli.

In trying to assess the results of swaddling, two considerations have to be borne in mind. First, infants were swaddled up to nine months, if not longer; second, the influence on development during the first year is difficult to reconstruct, though Lotte Dansiger and Liselotte Frankl have found that Albanian children outgrow the effects of a cradleboard very soon after its removal.

I venture to suggest that the effects of moderate swaddling are twofold. Once the narcissitic rind about the ego is removed, or as seen from the inside, the developing ego bursts out of its cocoon, a vacuum between self-interest and object-interest has to be filled. In anticipation of contact with the environment or object-world, as well as in actual contact, whether in a loving or frightening situation, the heart beats faster. This reaction is confirmed by the swaddling experiments of the American pediatricians, and it persists in the healthy adult. When the drives are freed from their shackles there must be expectation, anxiety and excitement, more danger, more pleasure through freer interaction with objects. Autoerotic activities may perhaps be pronounced because they assist in mastering the object hunger and gear the restrained body to satisfying contacts. Thus it is not surprising that object-relatedness did not manifest itself in the swaddled infant, particularly bearing in mind that the swaddled infant sleeps more than the free infant.

Can one go so far as to say that the psychology of infants, as we conceive of it since William Preyer's day (his infants were free), could not have been worked out unless swaddling had been given up? Furthermore, might it not change again—and this possibility is not ruled out by the American team of pediatricians—if infant rearing should revert one day to some form of swaddling?

Since the practice of swaddling has been discarded, the infant's narcissism has become exposed to new traumatization, perhaps to early strain or even injury and silent psychological trauma. Object-relatedness may appear earlier or prematurely and thus mislead the observer into speaking of primary object-love and not thinking of primary narcissism at all. Moreover—I would not like to bypass this observation—there was a generation of mothers and fathers, now perhaps grandmothers and grandfathers who had themselves been swaddled. Instead of repeating the tradition of their own infancy, and unaware of what had happened to them, they had perforce to rear their own infants in a manner quite unlike that laid down in their earliest memories. Here again we may be facing the problem of unconscious conflict solutions.

The concept of primary narcissism denotes the earliest state of mental organization. We assume that primary narcissism is not the product of a particular culture but of the earliest psychic processes operative in the undifferentiated state of mental organization. We revert to it in some degree in sleep-wakefulness cycles. We are roused from it through the mobility of cathexis between self- and object-sensations and representations and return to it to some extent when differentiation is being undone.

It will be evident from the title of this lecture and from my exposition that it has not been my intention to offer a coherent or comprehensive theory of early mental development. I do not think such a theory can be presented today. If and when it is formulated it will be as the result of the concerted effort of many workers. What I have tried to do is to share my experience with you. Just because of its obscurities, infancy is an exciting subject for the psychoanalyst, though possibly less appealing to the experimental psychologist.

PART II

PSYCHOANALYSIS AND THE EDUCATION OF THE CHILD

8

Group Formation in a School Community

This paper describes a children's society observed in the Baumgarten Home for three hundred orphans or semi-orphans, a home founded in Vienna by the American Joint Distribution Committee (cf. Bernfeld, 1921). The observations made by teachers and attendants on their daily round and the notes of leaders and members of this group yielded material that seemed worth making available in the interest of youth research. (It concerns a kind of military club, the Group, spontaneously formed by twenty boys between ten and sixteen years of age, together with one twenty-year-old and one twenty-two-year-old (the leader and author). The Group continued as such for five months. It grew out of an association of gymnasts which had formed itself a month earlier. When the leaders left the Home, the Group ceased to exist but this did not cause any break in the personal contact among leaders and members.

DATA AND METHODS

The data for this work were provided by (1) Observation, (2) Documents, (3) Statements, and (4) Statistics.

1. *Observation*. From its founding on October 15th, 1919 onward, observation of all events concerning both the Group as a whole and its individual members was carried on by the two leaders. (For ten weeks this was done without any specific aim.) Only on 1st January, 1920, did the author begin immediate registration of everything that happened, reproducing from memory some of the events of the earlier weeks.

2. *Documents*. In addition to the author's register, these consisted of a number of communications, drawings, and sketches done by the boys themselves, The Book of Work and the detailed Order-Book. This gives the names of those on duty and all orders, decrees, announcements, etc. It was kept by one of the boys as "clerk" and continued by the author when this boy left. A diary kept from 10th January to 25th February recorded all Group happenings in chronological order. A catalogue was also kept which registered observations on individual boys. The two together gave a comprehensive picture of the period covered.

3. *Statements*. These include both spontaneous statements and those resulting from a questionnaire, issued after the dissolution of the Group, which sought not only about personal data but also information about friendly relationships.

4. *Statistics*. Graphs and Tables omitted. (See Preface.) The main significance of the paper is the author's attempt to make the findings of psychoanalysis useful to youth research.

HISTORY

On 15th October, 1919, the American Aid Committee transferred three of Vienna's orphanages to part of a former military hospital in order to provide general assistance for two-hundred forty (later 300) oprhans, mostly refugees. These boys and girls, ranging in age from three to sixteen years and fairly well matched in age and sex, were assembled in the orphanages during the war years. The transfer to the new home was based partly on economic considerations but was also partly intended to raise the standard of orphan care to a higher social and educational level than hitherto customary. The children, neglected in body and mind by years of inhumane "refugee nurture," had become suspicious of and withdrawn from adults. The signs of disturbed emotional life that appeared after entry were not greatly surprising to their new supervisors. It did not escape notice that a group of twelve- to fourteen-year-olds surpassed the others in cunning and dexterity in obtaining a second helping at community meals. Intensive football, unlimited masturbation, and a compulsive urge to fight seemed to dominate their affective lives, which were only concentrated on food at meal times.

After a few days these children were given a "free constitution" by the adults in charge. The oldest (the fourteen- to sixteen-year-olds) took over part of the administration, appointed orderlies (twelve- to fourteen-year-olds) and began reluctantly to put the Home to rights, with adult advice. Although everyone was free to make decisions concerning his own life, he was never-the-less subject to the rules made by all in assembly and to the Court that they themselves instituted. These innovations resulted in a new psychological condition apparent even to the most naive observer. While most of these innovations were ignored, or even loudly rejected, by those under nine years old, in a few weeks time their effects were visible in the older children. Formerly adjusted to living on their own or in small groups, they now began to make contact with individuals, mainly with men or women teachers, slowly and mistrustfully but without obsequiousness. Their conversation consisted mostly of complaints about worn-out clothing and shoes, or too little to eat and, later, about persons who did not behave in the same way as the teachers who upheld the school community constitution. In this way individual teachers became friendly with single children or groups. The social content of these friendships was primitive and had little effect on the Home as a whole. The exception was a group of older boys, a "pupils' committee' who discussed Home affairs with the Director several evenings a week. At first no relationships were observed that were reminiscent of family or comradely ties. The only type of familiar seemed to be that denoted by 'Sir' which meant a person not only of authority but also of power.

The neglected state of the children shewed itself on entry. They dirtied and spoiled all their new clothing without a thought, and part of the equipment of the dining hall and school disappeared or was rendered useless within a few days. Water-closets were ignored, and it took the united efforts of the staff and some older girls to keep the Home even moderately sanitary.

Before breakfast on the second day the author, who acting as a teacher, asked some boys if they would like to do gymnastic exercises with him. Foty boys at once gathered round and readily obeyed a call to attention so that it was easy to get them into files. It was soon noticeable that if the leader made a file from the whole group, arranged in order of height, they stood quiet. If he allowed them to arrange themselves, he often had to witness a minor riot. It was obvious that the bigger boys wanted to stand together and didn't want any little ones in their section. The younger ones made no move to set up a file of their own but tried to get as near as possible to their seniors. After the fourth day, files were always ranged in order of height, brawling ceased, and courtesy reigned during exercise periods. Soon the files were divided into two squads, senior and junior, which exercised separately on account of their differing gymnastic ability. The juniors, however, seemed to prefer watching the seniors, who also drew many other spectators, including girls. This led to their calling themselves head-gymnasts; the author, hitherto the head-gymnanst, now became the leader. These seniors arrogated to themselves the right to walk about arm-in-arm wtih the leader during rest periods. These gymnastics were entirely voluntary and sometimes had to take place in the evening, but the seniors were keen to practice and rapidly improved. One day they locked the door to the exercise room and wanted to be watched only by people who knew something about gymnastics. This resulted in increased intimacy among the seniors and in a change in the leader's role. Whereas hitherto there had been complaints of "Mr. H., you are forever exercising with the juniors," now he belonged almost exclusively to the head-gymnasts, who liked to have him in their midst on every public occasion such as mealtimes, school assembly, Court sittings, etc. He was treated with greater confidence and consideration than most of the other adults, and the older boys themselves took over most of the exercising of the juniors.

So far three critical factors in the success of the program have emerged: (1) The exercises themselves, and their promotion of smartness, discipline, control, and so on; (2) the separation of seniors into a head-gymnast group or club associated with a) an increase in their prestige and b) the introduction of a social function, the taking over of the training of the juniors; and (3) the change in role of the leader who indeed was given complete authority over the head-gymnasts but was deliberately separated by them from the juniors.

These three developments make it easy to understand why some of the head-gymnasts sprang to the aid of those adults who were busy furnishing the Home. They said they did this "for love of the leader" and "because we are head-gymnasts." Any requested small services were willingly rendered but only to those who had a "decent" standard of behavior. Thus one sister was boycotted. Moving furtniture and other similar activities seemed very suitable for these boys at this time and allowed the gymnast club to extend its aims and take on a definite social function with the establishment of the Group, following discussions with leader about an "aid group."

The Order-Book initiated on 21 November gave particulars about the founding of "the voluntary aid battalions of the Baumgarten Childrens' Home." It arranged for the leader to be Inspector, for a head-gymnast to be "Crier" and for two gymnasts to be "orderlies-on-call." The Director took over as "Commander-in-Chief." The Home was exclusively Jewish and one fifteen-year-old, who had been a member of a scout organization "Haschomer" (Watchman) suggested the name Histradruth-Haschotrim (Watchman's Union), abbreviated from now on as H-H, and the use of Hebrew commando terms. The leader became "Manhig," the crier "Machris." Orderlies and part of the commando became "German for the time being."

The Order Book cited: "duty of the Marchris. The Marchris is instructed to begin his duties in the evening and to report to the

Inspector. He must make sure that none is roaming about within the precincts of the barracks and see that all windows are shut. Until a guard-room is set up he must go to bed at latest at eight-thirty. After breakfast he reports to the Commander and to the officer-in-charge, and betakes himself to class. After a guard room is set up" (this never happened) "the duties of the Machris will be altered." Franz (fifteen-years-old) kept the Order-Book and wrote it up himself, after occasional discussions with the Leader, until he left. He chose boys for duty from a list of members.

Orderlies-on-call were obliged "always to be ready when help was needed, to join in the evening round of the barracks, closing of windows etc. under the command of the Machris." The first entry in the Order-Book also contains many suggestions for the coming week," e.g., the setting up of a "Schotrim office" and provision of badges for the Machris and orderlies. In the evenings there was much talk about "service" and such vigorous practice of gymnastics that the leader had difficulty in restraining the boys from overdoing it. At his suggestion that number of orderlies was soon increased by three, following the Machris' complaint that "they are forever wanting to join the patrol." This duty was carried out perfectly, the boys themselves keeping check on it. The other inhabitants of the Home were not officially notified of the existence of the Group.

On the third day, the leader himself wrote an order: "The Machris can investigate all youngsters who leave the Home carrying parcels. The consent of the School Committee must be obtained. If anyone is stopped, the Inspector must be informed as soon as possible." When the Home first opened there was much theft. The boys had themselves proposed that "something should be done about it." In this way, the H-H took the first step to overcoming it. At the next session of the School Committee, the Leader reported the formation of the H-H and obtained permission for the continuance of their duties, including the inspection of parcels. The Committee decided that parcels belonging to girls or staff should also be inspected. During the permitted hours of exit, two orderlies were stationed at the door to examine parcels. In this way it was confirmed that a member of the kitchen staff was carrying away bread etc. That evening the Machris asked the leader to obtain directives from the management. From 24 November on, all tasks were announced at roll-call and called "achievements" at the request of Emil. At an evening discussion Richard contended that there was a difference between a job done wholly voluntarily or one done simply because it was the duty of a Schoter. The former were called "high style achievements" to distinguish them from ordinary "achievements."

An incident made it necessary to inform inhabitants who were not members of the School Committee of the formation of the Group. The Manager of the Home one day asked the second elected leader, Mr. F., if the boys could make urgently needed beds and straw mattresses. The Machris assembled the boys and they carried out the work. But when the Manager offered them an extra portion of bread as a reward, the boys refused it because, as Richard said angrily later, "We only work of our own free will and do not need anything for it." Further work for the Manager was declined for a long time afterward.

Pilfering still continued and on 20 November, the Group held a very private meeting at which the boys themselves asked for strong measures. Strict inspection was to continue but all were to be constantly on the watch. The Machris claimed as his right that "if anyone is caught, he must be informed at once and he alone have the right to come to any decision." Several people, including unpopular adults, were suspected as well as those children who had been found guilty in earlier Homes or were "capable" of stealing.

The supervisors and the H-H kept order in the Home, the latter being entrusted with special tasks. On 25 November the dining-room supervisor complained that three of the Schotrim were interfering with his functions. Next day the Order-Book read "The service of the Schotrim is strictly limited to the area outside the barracks. No Schotrim may enter the barracks on duty." When badges were given out to those on duty, the Machris asked for a torch for use on evening rounds. Whistles were requested so that in case of trouble they could make themselves heard. Richard wanted caps, gloves, and sweaters for orderlies-on-call. On 2 December, Emil told the leader that a youngster who had just entered the Home had saved the life of a woman on a tram and should therefore immediately become a Schoter, and be rewarded in some way. The leader suggested that they should either give the boy (Fritz) the title of Machris in perpetuity or arrange a celebration in his honor. The Machris idea met with opposition, and eventually the celebration was approved, though in fact it never took place. During the discussion, the rating of tasks was again raised, and it was agreed that jobs taking several hours should be called "operations" and really big undertaking "deeds." Fritz's action in preventing a severe accident was to be considered a "deed."

H-H services increased daily. The boys compiled the sicklist and delivered it to the school office. On 4 December the living-room of some resident fourteen- to sixteen-year-old apprentices had to be inspected because one of them was "trading in food." On the same day whistles were distributed to all Schotrim. There had been exercises almost every evening, and preparations were now made for a gymnastic display on an upcoming holiday. It did not take place because one of the leaders was absent—a failure that was held against him for a long time. When several members left the Home to go abroad, several juniors were taken in as a "Second Troop" on probation for two weeks (Order-Book, 23 December). In the course of the month, a big cross-country excursion took place which the boys talked about for months afterwards, two members, Richard and Emil, were elected to the School Committee; and the issuing of week-day exit permits was allotted to the Machris. The arrival of many deprived and dirty children from a refugee camp drew close attention from members. The pilfering and disappearance of food, which had almost entirely ceased, now began again, and as a result still stricter vigilance was enforced. From time to time, the Machris reported successful investigations of thefts.

The new Schotrim on probation had to write on a slip of paper the name of the senior to whom they wished "to render service." In January, apart from bigger "operations," nothing happened worth reporting. The most noticeable development was the marked increase in the authority of the H-H. The Diary describes one big "operation" on 25 and 26 January, namely the removal of a tailoring workship with its sewing machines, presses, etc., moved to a new site. Squads of five, each with a leader, made it their business to do the job as quickly as possible, with only the leaders being allowed to speak. The work was finished in 25 minutes. Then the leading boy collected the others and marched them, singing, to their dormitory. Work next day began early. The Leader, by request, woke all the Schotrim before the usual time so that they could begin punctually. They worked from half-past seven to nine o'clock and again from nine-thirty to ten-thirty. During the break they gathered round the Leader as usual and much discussion ensued about putting up a partition in the living-room behind which the Machris could issue his exit permits, about the much-desired uniforms and camping equipment, and so on. Some of the boys were tired when work ended and football was arranged for eleven thirty, but, some of the new Second Troop was asked to go on working even after eleven. They only did what they were told by the Leader or by the seniors, whereas the First Troop arranged and carried out their tasks independently.

On 1 February the Machris was sorting out items which had been stolen or found, which he wanted to hand over to the management. The Leader asked him 'What are you going to do about the brushes and combs?' He replied: "Well, I suppose we might as well give them to the management too." Leader: "Would it not be better to give them direct to the girls in barrack 29? They have none." Machris: "No, not the girls under any circumstances. See, we have none ourselves either. Why should the girls have everything? Moreover we have confiscated them." Leader: "That's true, but the girls need them more than you do because they have longer hair. Will you perhaps hand them over to the H-A to issue?" Machris: "That's fine." The H-A (Histadruth Hist-Avodah) was a girls' organization set up after the formation of the H-H, to provide services like darning, etc. It developed on much the same lines as the boys' Group and came to have similar standing in the Home.

Every evening in early February the boys asked for exercises and for patrols in the open air. One night a small troop led by Emil set out in advance, left the path and, hidden by the darkness, ambushed the next two squads. Such independent behavior was now frequent.

On 4 and 5 February the existence of the Group was threatened for the first time. The H-A arranged a party for the evening of the fourth to which they invited the leaders but not all the boys. When they heard about this they spontaneously decided that all or none should go and, when the time came, they all marched in to the party.

Next day Emil and Richard complained bitterly to the Leader that they had been insulted as Schotrim by a girl who apparently said "Thank God," as they were leaving. Indignant remarks were made such as "the Schotrim are slaves," "we have no standing in Baumgarten," etc., and the Leader was asked to write to the girls demanding atonement and respect. That evening a nursing sister made a personal apology on behalf of the girls. The boys were still upset, but, after a long discussion with the Leader and a cross-country run, the incident was not mentioned again.

On the evening of 20 February, an hour before the official Friday ceremony, the H-H undertook the unloading of a delivery of coal and wood. Several nonmembers offered to help but were vigorously rejected; only Schotrim were to work. When the job was finished in two hours time, the ceremony was over and a special ceremony was arranged.

Later, owing to the illness of the Director and several teachers, the Home underwent a sixteen-day crisis during which the leaders were so much in demand that they had little time for the H-H. The boys' resentment of this neglect came to a head when it was announced that boys who had left for Holland in November were shortly coming back with demands for "daily orders," etc., the usual routine having lapsed. With the return of the seven boys from abroad, the usual roll-call, exercises, evening discussions, and readings were re-established. The allocation of beds for the returned members caused pressing demands for a separate dormitory for the H-H.

One Friday evening, about twenty emigrants from Palestine interested the boys with their singing and dancing. The H-H wanted a similar display to be given in their room, which had at last been put to rights. Here, with windows shrouded and doors locked, the leaders had had to tell tales of their adventures. The communal life of the boys both among themselves and with the leaders became steadily more intimate and intense. Every midday or evening there were patrols and exercises, relay races (always between the First Troop and the Second), and other activities. Daily too there were conferences with individuals or groups about work, status, above all about excursions, combined with daydreams about all the much desired equipment. The greater part of these daydreams were never realized. Though the Group was nearing its dissolution, there is little to record about its last weeks, during which its vitality seemed greater than ever.

STRUCTURE OF THE GROUP AS A WHOLE

After the institution of communal gymastics in October, 1919, sixteen boys exercised regularly of their own free will. They became the head-gymnasts and the First Troop of the Group. Three new members were admitted on 15 November. After some of the group left for Holland, their number was quickly restored by the admission of younger boys, i.e., by the formation of the Second Troop. The expulsion of three boys on probation on 21 January reduced the group's members to sixteen, but the loss was made up by the intake of four more into the Second Troop. Thus for more than two months the Group had a membership of about twenty, and the number increased to its maximum of twenty-six when the travellers came back.

The senior members (15-to 16-years-old) completely dominated the juniors (13- to 14-years-old). They were reluctant to admit younger members, preferring boys of greater age, height, and strength. Thus the Second Troop was only enrolled when the exodus to Holland made it necessary for the continuance of adequate service. This seems to prove that the Group was best suited to the older boys and confirms the findings of youth research that boys' societies tend to have specific physical or mental characteristics. Certainly age and height were the most important criteria for acceptance or refusal of new members. After the departure of seniors to Holland and the intake of smaller boys, the average height of members dropped considerably, with only two taller boys, Rudolf and Emil, remaining. In addition to age and height, health and strength were criteria for admission. Bodily infirmity was the reason the three boys were expelled in January. Physical factors were also involved. In addition to criticisms like, "he is so small," boys made remarks such as "He is always lazy," "He is stupid," "He doesn't do what he is told." The stress laid on being good, keeping order, being guided by the seniors in the initiation of new members was reflected in remarks made about seniors during their absence abroad: "Smart Eric," "When Bruno was Machris, everything was all right," "Bruno inspected everything—when it was windy I used to go round with him shutting windows."

The deliberate separation of the seniors and juniors by their being split into head-gymnasts and gymnasts doubtless conduced to the formation of the Group. The younger boys simply could not do all the exercises of which the older ones were capable. The characteristics of gymnastic ability, a degree of intelligence and self-control, and pleasure in rhythm and in exercising together came to be desiderata in the Group and to result in intensification of such activities as, excursions and patrols. The military aspect of the Group, "playing at soldiers," is not to be explained as mere "imitation." It seems to me that such imitation requires a particular psychic constellation to bring it into operation, whereas the structure of the Group was not a constant; it became modified both by changes in membership and by increasing contact with leaders and other adults.

During the head-gymnast period (October-November) the most important criterion seemed to be the ability to render service. It remains an open question whether the boys chose members to fill jobs or whether they arranged jobs first to serve as tests of suitability. Certainly anyone capable of service was valued. Thus both the work of the Machris (walking, calling to meals, leading orderlies) and that of the orderlies (helping when needed, going on evening patrol, etc.) were highly esteemed, as was communal service, including roll-call and gymnastics. "To belong to the Schotrim" i.e., to be recognized by the first closed Group in the Home was the foremost aim of the other children. Permission to exericse seemed to be equivalent to reognition of physical ability. When the Group was given official recognition, the close association with the Leaders showed itself, often ostentatiously, by members walking arm in arm, or making arrogant remarks to juniors in public. The relationship with the Leaders later became more genuinely friendly.

When a leader spoke to a boy, the boy spontaneously stood at attention. They always came to help in cleaning-up operations, never failing to make themselves conspicuous or to point out how well they did their work. Personal relationships grew out of working together and out of the common interests of boys and leaders. A group of four boys in particular accompanied the leaders whenever they could and talked to them about many things concerning the Home as well as the Group itself. The admission of juniors was constantly discussed, but, though many youngsters sought admission, no junior was accepted until 21 December.

The distribution of badges to office-holders and of whistles to all members had interesting results It soon became apparent that non-members had acquired whistles. At Richard's instigation the School community passed a motion restricting the ownership and use of whistles to the Schotrim, who wore them on cords on their jackets. They decided that any member going abroad must give up his whistle the evening before he went away; it would be kept for them on their return. Two boys sent theirs back from the railway station. These Group badges gave additional stimulus to wishful fantasies in discussions among themselves and with Leaders. Shorts and shirts, and a kind of scout "Schotrim uniform" were much in demand. These longings showed little regard for practical considerations: thus shoes were never mentioned though these were badly needed, since the boys had to practice in bare feet or wooden-soled shoes. In December, Richard sketched a green armband with a central double eagle which he suggested should replace the current black-striped one. It is characteristic that, after the formation of the Group, wishes for uniforms and camping equipment increased in number and scope. As standards of achievement grew higher (e.g., Fritz's "deed"), conditions of admission to membership became even stricter, any form of dishonesty being cause of rejection. Much debate occurred about whether a member who had been found guilty of pilfering should be expelled. It was decided to punish him by depriving him of his whistle, thus branding him as a potential thief.

Group life, as dintinct from the initial gymnast club, underwent considerable modification after the intake of juniors on 21 December. Its chief features until then will now be summarized. (1) The close linkage of members showed itself in:

a) Behavior. Working together as an openly acknowledged function of the Group; raising its status by making work a monopoly, voting together in school community, making conditions of entry difficult.

b) Wishes for clearer distinction from other inmates, by means of uniforms, separate bed- and duty-rooms, closer friendships with each other and leaders, use of "thou" and Christian names.

c) Moral demands for honesty, adherence to school community rules, readiness to help. Also more aesthetic and hygienic demands for personal cleanliness and cleanliness of clothing and of premises, especially the privies. On a more social level, unconditional trustworthiness was sought in mutual relationships of members. Demands differed from wishes by the frequency of their expression and the measures taken to see that they were fulfilled.

(2) The unity of the Group as distinct from non-members can be seen in the near uniformity of most members in:

a) physical characteristics, i.e., preference for older, taller, and stronger members, none with any physical deficiency being admitted.

b) psycho-physical characteristics required for the successful conduct of work, as formerly required by gymnast club—i.e., endurance, resitance to fatigue, muscular control etc. Clumsiness often put the mentally agile at a disadvantage with the physically more dexterous and nimble.

c) mental characteristics. Intellectural ability does not seem to have been a criterion for admission. Remarks like "he is so stupid," referred to general inferiority—not specifically intellectual incapability—on the part of an applicant. Members were of one school type, distributed between four classes so that differences never became important, and we never noticed any significant difference among them. The focus of the Group was an affective one, as shown by the pleasure with which all its functions were approached, as well as the strength of friendships, wishes, and demands. The translation of demands into reality created a kind of Group sentiment. The Group becoming regarded as an association of boys who were honest, clean, helpful, and self-sacrificing. It was this image that many younger boys tried unsuccessfully to live up to. Similarity in emotional life (including similar infantile and pre-pubertal drives) seemed to be essential for membership.

From 21 November to 21 December this firmly closed association, with definite standards of value, postulated certain rights in the Home, partly owing to its physical power (all the boys were strong) and partly to its moral-social advantages. These two factors, conferring power status, could operate singularly or together; that is, non-members could be brutally treated by workers or actively helped out of difficulties.

Important events occurred during the five days December 20-25. There was a celebration in the Home during which the Group rendered extensive service, and their awareness of power and solidarity vis-a-vis the other inmates reached its zenith.

Their courier activites, especially the fetching of guests from the station in cars, was a frequent topic for conversation.

The second event was the departure of eight members abroad which resulted in overburdening the remaining members. Duties rotated so quickly that the badges of office-holders tended to lose value and there were disruptions of friendships. Hence finally it was agreed to admit younger boys, a decision instigated by the Director and by Leader F. Selected by the members themselves, ten boys were accepted; three "weaklings" were expelled after two days, and the remaining seven were retained on probation. These novices formed the Second Troop and served as orderlies-on-call, being allowed badges on duty but not whistles. The seniors subjected them to a kind of military training. During exercises they were somtimes rather roughly treated. However when they chose the individual older boy to whom they wished to be attached for service, he was expected to look after their welfare and give them any help required. The essential demand on the Second Troop was, therefore, for obedience and docility. The First Troop was always in command and took all the initiative in work and other activities.

The uniformity of the Group in age and height was now destroyed, and its cohesion threatened to some extent by the lesser physical capacity of the young probationers. The Group still cohered, partly because of the younger boys' devotion to work, their willingness to submit to the command of their seniors, and their fervent desire to live up to the standard of Schotrim. Juniors were always well-treated by seniors in public and sometimes given preferential treatment over non-members. Richard, who was a judge, announced that any Second Trooper who appeared before the School Court would be severely punished. The unity of the Group as a whole may be said to have been cemented by the reciprocal relations between the two Troops—the First commanding, the Second obeying—and by the common interest in work, exercise, and excursions.

When familiarity increased, personal friendships developed between older and younger boys, and the behavior of seniors during leisure hours was often very different from that during work periods. During work periods, though juniors could be reprimanded and corrected, they were also praised when they did well and encouraged by such appreciation of their efforts. The new entrants felt that the expulsion of three of them as unsuitable strengthened their own position as potential schotrim. Thus, in spite of changes in the association owing to the formation of the Second Troop, the solidarity of the Group towards outsiders was never impaired.

THE LEADERS AND THEIR RELATION TO THE BOYS

Biographical data submitted to the Director showed that, in spite of their ages (22 and 20) both Leader H. (the author) and Leader F. had had ample experience as members and organizers of boy's clubs. Leader H. quickly became at home with his gymnasts and later with the members of the Group. At the time he had had no pedagogic training and used to special methods, believing that merely being with boys of a certain age allows us to "exert greater mutual influence on one another than do others in the environment." Apart from directing the gymastic exercises, his role as leader was confined to making suggestions which the boys could carry out or not as they wished and to discussing all problems with them. Both leaders agreed about the personal characteristics that advanced their standing the Group i.e., height and strength, intelligence, agility and manner of giving commands.Understanding of what mattered to the boys, availability at all times when help was needed, and approppriate behavior to those on duty formed the basis of the leaders' standing. The boys attached great value to whatever intimacies the leaders allowed. If a boy was insolent, they played the role of injured victim so that the offender soon came and apologized of his own accord.

Authoritative relations were established voluntarily by the free choice of the boys. When gymnastics began, the teacher knew little about the boys but fortunately hit upon the right approach. They were eager to exercise and wanted to be firmly handled, sometimes even provoking correction. A boy might fail to obey unless threatened with expulsion or some such "severe punishment."

This authority soon proved a social necessity. Instead of kicking plaster off the walls and doing other damage, some boys could be induced to practice walking on stilts, to climb trees, or to organize competitive races. The precise form of the occupation did not seem to matter, only the pleasure gain from satisfaction of drives. By such means the authority of the gymnastic teacher rendered these drive-activities socially positive.

The foundation of the Group and the resulting work of the boys for the Home brought them into much closer and more frequent contact with the leaders, even for as much as several hours every day. The leaders were charged with the administrative management of the Group, since the participation of the Director, unanimously elected as Commander-in-Chief, was purely formal. Very soon the boys established friendly relations with the leaders, walking about with them arm-in-arm and asking trustful questions or requesting advice about personal concerns. These friendly relations did not impair the authority of the Leaders, especially in the gymnastic exercises. Indeed, the wish "to be managed" always found fresh expression. Some boys kept close to the leaders during service periods or leaned up against them during discussions. If the leaders left the Home they were often accompanied for some distance. Richard and Emil used to confide in them. At sessions of the School Community the leaders were called to join the Group members. Indeed, every opportunity was taken to proclaim "ownership" of the leaders by the Group. Relations deepened when a room was allotted to the Group, the Schotrim's room. Here the leaders spent nearly every evening, talking or reading aloud. The friendship accorded them was not extended to any of the other adults. During one roll-call, Richard handed the Leader a drawing of a star of David, decorated with leaves, signed by thirteen members and inscribed to their Mannig, 'This heart is watched over by the Schotrim'. A rather similar drawing, probably also Richard's, read, "Long live our Mannig H.. and F...".

Very few instances of aversion from or resentment toward the leaders were observed. Once, when Emil's attention was drawn to incorrect drilling of six juniors, he waved his hand in rejection, saying testily, "Do leave me alone, I know all about it." The most marked incentive to rejection by the Group was the insult by the girls that raised such a storm of anger and resentment and occasioned remarks like "Mr. H., you don't care about us any more. We are no longer smart and neither are you." These feelings were reversed after discussion with the leaders and apology from the girls. There was never any rebellion during work, even when demands were irksome.

FRIENDSHIPS AMONG THE BOYS

At first the need for communal friendship took precedence over relations between individuals, though the Machris's choice of members for duty, and his inquiries (such as "Who wants to come on patrol with X?") conveyed hints of personal preferences. Remarks such as "I was with you yesterday. That was fine. Come along today too," were heard when squads formed spontaneously for work, offers of mutual help could be heard. Sometimes two boys were found in one bed. This was forbidden by the dormitory orderlies, but the boys justified it by saying, "It is too cold by oneself," "There are not enough blankets," etc. Gideon regularly lay with his brothers, Robert with his brother and later with Jacob. It seemed to happen with boys of eleven and under rather than with older ones. Robert and Jacob were a special case. At the end of February Marcus reported that Robert, a founder, had left the Group; no one could say why, but a woman teacher said a few days later that Robert and a new entrant, 12-year-old Jacob, nicknamed "Mopsi," had been inseparable for some days, always sitting together, kissing and stroking each other. Robert and Jacob remained close friends. This was the only instance in which such a close personal relationship was observed. Regard for the Leaders was shown by naming garden beds after them. When groups formed spontaneously for reading aloud or for games requiring two sides, unpopular boys would be ejected or pushed across to the other side.

In the Questionnaire sent out after the dissolution of the Group, each boy was asked "Did you have a friend or friends among the Schotrim" and, if so, "who were they?". Twenty-two boys answered in the affirmative, one after some delay and only one in the negative. There was some hesitation about citing names. Those collected fell into three categories—best friends, good friends, and friends. There were 33 names in the first group, 25 in the second, and only 9 in the third. It emerged that most of the cited friendships were unreciprocated. Indeed, there were only eight pairs of mutual friends—six between seniors, two between seniors and juniors, and none at all between juniors. Seniors both named more friends and were named more often than juniors. Richard was named nine times and himself named eight friends. This showed him to be in contact with most of the members so that he served as an intermediary, bringing other boys into relationship through their friendship for him. Emil and Werner were each named three times; they were very good mutual friends with Richard. Philip, Jacob, and Marcus were the most popular among the juniors, especially with the seniors. Seven boys were not named as friends, but only one said he had no friends. As implied earlier, most friendships were less overt than that between Jacob and Marcus but could be inferred from choice of companions in work or play.

THE TROOPS

The energies of the Group were united and anchored in the First Troop, which comprised two subgroups. One consisted of the leaders and the boys Emil, Richard, Rudolf, Markus, and Simon in order of precedence established by observation together with Franz, Bruno, and a few others. The other subgroup consisted of boys who attached themselves more or less singularly. Richard and Emil were centers of activity, were regarded as representatives of the Group, and were both made members of the School Committee. Richard set the tone in all discussions and had great influence. Simon was friendly with the Leaders but less so with other boys, except Emil. Observation revealed Karl's undoubted dislike of Emil, for which no basis was ever clear, Marcus, after weeks of spiteful hatred of Simon became reconciled to him, saying to a leader that Emil wished this and that 'in the H-H everyone should be on good terms.' Enmity was even more difficult to establish by observation than was friendship.

The subgrouping of members returning from their visit to Holland was not easy to determine. Founding members Max, Bruno, Franz and Aaron did not come back till after the dissolution. Others, who returned in time to rejoin, had no obvious influence. Complete reabsorption into the Group took time, though Rudolf, as the tallest and strongest, had a status midway between member and leader. He had neither many friends nor much observable influence but always exercised authority during service activities.

There was less variation in the Second Troop. Stringent methods of choice (stemming from the boys and not from the leaders) presupposed complete dependence of juniors on such majority agreement of seniors. All concurred in promoting obedience, and service ability increased. No similar incident occurred after the expulsion of the three "weaklings" in January. Adolf was the only junior ever to be admitted to the First Troop after 8 weeks on probation. Six seniors named him as a friend, two saying, "I liked him very much." The decisive characteristic of the Second Troop can be summarized as submission to the seniors as and when required. They rather resembled the earlier gymnast club in their enthusiasm for exercises and adventures, always in pursuit of appreciation from the seniors.

THE HOME AND THE GROUP

It was evident, even before the founding of the Group, that the resident adults fell into two sections according to their attitudes and behavior toward the youngsters. One section, chiefly teachers and helpers, maintained a patient attitude toward the boys' activities.

Thus, for example, they took the annoyance of luggage inspection as much for granted as the boys. These adults were pleased about the founding of the Group. The other section maintained the more critical attitude reflected in the constitution and management of the Home. Among the Group, however, nothing was ever said about any member of this section, and small services were rendered them. As mistrust disappeared with further contact, the boys acquired a more personal interest in the adults. Thus a dispute with the director of the workshop, whose affection was assured, was so conducted that he himself was not condemned though a measure he had instituted was severly criticized. No boy was ever known to lie to an adult (for pedagogic implications see Bernfield, 1921).

The first section encouraged the Group in their pursuit of power. The second did not disapprove so long as the boys did not require more than thanks for services rendered. As the Home became better established, and as the need for services diminished, along with a steady increase in the boys' estimation of their own work, their tolerance decreased. Some gave evidence of their own power, for example, by showing preference in the distribution of laundry. If the need for service did arise, the boys would be courteously asked for help, but immediately after the work was done they were subjected again to the treatment usually accorded to orphans. Clearly their work was more highly valued than was the Group itself. With its controls, inspections, and demands for regulations to which adults were also required to confrom, the Group was more hated and cursed than admired as the boys expected it to be. Things came to a head with the incident related in the "History" when the Manager's offer of extra bread was angrily resented as an affront, after which all service to the management ceased for a long time. The boys only gave voluntary service to people they liked, often provoking earnest pleading from persons of whose affection they were not sure. Marcus (aged fourteen) was asked by a nurse to fetch coal in a not too friendly manner. He refused, whereupon the nurse reminded him he was a 'Schoter'. After thinking this over Marcus said "I'll do it, not because I am a Schoter but because I don't want it to be so cold in your room as it is in our dormitory." Nevertheless, the best way to get boys to do jobs for adults was usually to appeal to their membership of the Group. No special privileges were accorded to adults; the boys continued to treat them in the same reserved, though not insulting, manner as they did the rest of the children in the Home.

These other children became aware of the original gymnast group because it provided exercises they could watch. The founding of the Group resulted in their watching training sessions as they had watched the gymnastics. "Roll-call" drew their attention. None laughed at the Hebrew in which commands were given. Some of the smaller boys who were forever trying to become members, asked about the meaning of these words and used them correctly in their imitative games. Spectators often tried to carry out these commands themselves. Mastery of an exercise, approved by a member or leader, was regularly followed by a request for admission. A group of eight- to twelve-year-old girls also followed the exercises but caused disturbance when the exercises became too difficult for them. A rule of the School Community then ordered that "The Schotrim should not be disturbed while exercising." These tiresome girls were disliked, but all the others received little attention. These eighty to one hundred girls were partly benevolent (as in forming their own group to render services like darning) and partly indifferent to the Group, not feeling it had much to do with them. Until the quarrel after the girl's party, however, their conceding to all the privileges and concurring the regulations of the School Community was considered by the boys as evidence of the required approval, subordination, and admiration. The Group's behavior to the girls varied according to circumstances—from near brutality if they did not get out of the way quickly when the boys were working or failed to open a door submissively to a kind of knight-errantry and showing off during exercises and at other times.

Observation confirmed that the boys who did not belong to the Group were dominated by the urge to become members. The little boys were willing to be commanded by the Group and rendered the obligatory obedience in the hope of achieving entry. This strong positive relationship was quite different from their comparatively non-existent one with the girls.

For four months the Group made use of this situation,

strengthening its authority by its mere existence and by its work, and gradually winning over all the male inmates. But at the beginning of March (fifth month), a second power group emerged. Three fifteen-to sixteen-year-old boys, who had never liked the militaristic form of the Group, bestirred themselves to deepen interest in the School Community and to bring its authority, hitherto only partial, to bear directly on the group. However, on account of the standing of the leaders in the Home and the presence of Richard and Emil on the School Community, open warfare between the two groups seemed unlikely, and the existence of the Group was held to be secure and socially useful.

General Psychological Observations on the Group's Development

The Group underwent significant changes in a short time. That we are dealing here with a psychically determined phenomenon is supported by the conclusions of child psychology that at least one form of children's association, namely that undertaken for play, is so determined. Whether, apart from the former scout who named the Group, any of the boys had earlier been members of associations could not be determined. Their uncivilized behavior on arrival spoke against this, though their passion for football and some small pilfering groups spoke for it, if only for occasional, short periods. At first the wish to practice gymnastics implied no need for working together or for companionship; there were many instances of inconsiderate behavior to fellow gymnasts. But the preference of the older boys for working together and of the younger ones for getting as close as they could to their seniors soon showed itself. It was gymnastics as such that was foremost in their minds. For the teacher, this meant their standing still, only moving when ordered. For the boys it meant being told what to do, sometimes reprimanded, but above all, being asked to give unqualified obedience. These wishes to be controlled were further gratified by repetitions outside exercise hours, when commanded by a Group member. "Standing to attention," actually requested only during gymnastics, was voluntarily extended to meetings with the teacher outside the exercise room and even to the school. Play theorists (cf. Groos,

1910) regard football as the expression of a drive to fight. In the gymnastics the drive seemed less aggressive, more simply directed to the pleasure of rhythmic movement. Football and gymnastics seemed to remain side by side as complementary but satisfactory forms of expression. Though the wish for control dominated the first period of exercises, the head-gymnasts soon developed a more positive attitude: they began to instigate and wish to lead exercises, to think up new ones, and to command younger boys, but retained throughout their passive obedience to the teacher. With this mixture of ages and abilities among the gymnasts, and given the often ineffectual attempts of seniors to command juniors, who not infrequently laughed at their efforts, little progress was made until the separating off of the head-gymnasts and their arrogation of the teachers (now leaders) to themselves excluded all juniors from their exercise periods. Failure to control the little ones began to induce greater self-control. Leaders were still essentially a means to an end—the mastery of exercises—but more personal friendly relations now developed. A certain resentment by some of the better gymnasts at being corrected in front of the little ones now resolved itself. Exercise ceased to be agreeable play and became more like serious work, any attempt to make fun of it being reprimanded by the boys themselves. Esteem for the Leaders increased as the drive to real mastery emerged alongside fantasied wish-fulfillment: The leader became the wish-object. What Monroe (1899) proved about American children—i.e. that their wish object must represent what they themselves would like to be but are not—applied in this case.

As noted earlier, the head-gymnasts formed the nucleus of the Group; its first labors were directed to improving its own image and thus rendering a service to the leaders. The sense of power associated with training the little boys showed itself also in their attitude to heavy work. Both tasks seemed to give more pleasure the more urgent the demand and the more ruthless towards themselves and their objectives the Group members were allowed to be. The assumption that altruistic drives towards the Home were already active does not seem justified. Though definite advantages accrued to the Home through their work and its social effects, it was clear that their actions were directed to obtaining appreciation, esteem and high valuation from all the inmates. The egoistic drives showed a change in their forms and ways of expression, many of the Group's activities directly promoting socialization. Soon the boys' emotions became milder and more refined. Imitation of the leaders' behavior seemed more and more to take the place of identification. A real effort to be like them replaced the fantasied wish-fulfillment of being the same.

Though wishes to please and to be needed met with considerable success, material wishes for uniforms, and camping equipment were unfulfilled. In the evenings spent with the Leaders the boys sometimes wished there were more members in the group, daydreaming about the disposition of troops. But their close union, and their monopolization of the leaders and of work militated against these wishes, as is shown by the severity of their criteria for admission of big as well as small boys. When juniors were admitted, it seemed rather as an attempt to preserve the glory of a unique twenty-member Group than to provide better service to the Home. After extended probation and the dismissal of "weaklings," only one boy was promoted from the Second to the First Troop. With the intake of juniors, the desire to rule re-emerged but in a milder form: the youngsters were to be ruled but also trained and helped when necessary. They were participants in a common egoistic aim—maintaining the status of the Group.

The influence of the adults in the Home on the Group and its relations with them varied according to whether they belonged to the section which was encouraging and helpful or to the section which was critical and sometimes antagonistic. When trouble occurred with the latter, the leaders were called on to act as liaison officers, a role in which they were on the whole successful, though the boys were naturally easier to deal with than the offended adults. The boys' attitude to the encouraging adults soon became, and remained, positive, because those adults helped them to realize their wishes so far as conditions allowed, without setting unwanted limits to their activities. Relations with this section soon overcame the children's initial resistance to all adults, though they continued to mistrust anyone of whose approval they were unsure and were hard to convince if one of these adults wished to become friendly. Any serious disturbance, like the Manager's offer of extra bread, that offended their sense of dignity or seemed to threaten the status of the Group, could reawaken their suspicions of all adults, including even, temporarily, the leaders. But these two sections of adults afforded an element of tension from which the Group derived its resistance and appetite for power, as well as feelings of satisfaction and fulfillment of wishes. Had not both sections existed, the one might have converted the Group activities into a kind of game, whereas the other might have permitted too much wish-realization, so that the hallucinatory part of their action, characteristic of children and young people, might have been lost.

Only the School Community in assembly could legitimately oppose the Group's wishes but this only happened once, when they interfered with the functions of the dining-room manager. By contrast, the School Committee, which conducted the Home, twice expressed doubts to the Manager, once about the militarization of the Group endangering democracy and later when the children showed an ever livelier participation in the School Assembly. The members did appear to constitute a closed group, voting unanimously whenever the agenda concerned matters like holidays and gardening in which the Group members arrogated to themselves priority over the others. They regarded themselves rather as superior to the Community, whereas the boys who later instigated a rival "Union for Work" wanted to see them as just one link in a harmonious School Community. The egoism of the Group made such a transition difficult. Their psychic structure opposed any such transition from "I" to "Thou." Although we never observed any evidence of altruistic trends, the Group was nevertheless socially advantageous to the Home.

A Psychoanalytic View of the Group Process

A deeper understanding of the Group is afforded by the findings of psychoanalysis. When the children first arrived in the Home both the service staff (and some youngsters) and the teachers complained bitterly about their behavior, the former about their lack of cleanliness, fouling of clothing and lavatories, and bed-wetting, and the latter about destruction of books and equipment, viciousness, and belligerence. Football was the only activity in which they showed any kind of social behavior, though even there, play was excessively rough. Some of the boys were found in bed in pairs. We never discovered whether or what fantasies accompanied the frequent masturbatory activities, usually carried out by individuals on their own, but in which 6- to 10-year-olds also took part.

Primary infantile sexual activites (coprophilia, sadomasochistic drives, etc.) were still observable. Censorship and repression seemed to be lacking. Civilized ways of behavior seemed as alien to most of the boys as to a newborn baby. They must have heard about these one way or another but they lacked any impetus to cultivate them. The prospect of preferential treatment or friendship with a teacher did not promise to compensate for the sacrifice of infantile pleasures.

Judging by the vigor with which they practiced and their willingness to obey orders, it seemed that the gymnasts were dominated at first by sado-masochistic drives though others were already active, probably even the genital drive itself. The significant thing about the later Group is that it only changed in any direction when some of its members entered a new phase together.

After the separation of seniors and juniors for pactice, ego drives seemed to predominate among the head-gymnasts, as evidenced by the monopolization of the leaders etc. These ego drives may have been supported by sexual drives (Freud, 1914) but the latter seemed to appear independently. The head-gymnasts enjoyed themselves more on their own. That the separation from the juniors they demanded had something to do with a higher valuation of their own genitals cannot be ruled out.

The firm establishment of the Group and its functions, the regard shown by the other children, and the pleasure to be derived in exercise through self-command, resulted in a libido fixation to their own ego "analogous to the first autoerotic sexual gratification that exists in association with life furthering functions of self preservation" (Freud, 1914). This libido fixation is secondary, i.e., it has a newly discovered self for its aim, as distinct from its infantile narcissistic object. This fixation was not unconditional; the new self had to conform to certain standards, in short to an ego-ideal. An ego-ideal can only contribute to the formation of a society if the individuals concerned have some features in common—in this case age, height, strength, willingness to work, and so on.

This Group ego-ideal was formed because the personal egos of its members could no longer keep pace with cultural requirements of the Home (Freud, 1914), and even the sadomasochistic gratification of exercising became questionable because of shortcomings and failures in taking command. It came about through awareness of what the personal ego lacked and what it wanted to be, and it resulted in the onset of repression of those impulses not in accord with it. Out of the sadistic desire to command (often wrongly) came the wish to be able to command well, thereby obtaining not only personal satisfaction but the approval of the leader. Repression served to elevate the ego and to win the sexual love-object (the leader). What he called "bad" and disliked must be set aside; what he approved must be practiced and manifested.

The persons of the leaders played a substantial part in the formation of the ego-ideal. At first only facilitators, they later became objects of homosexual libido, which had to be invested in the ego-ideal. Their persons served as the standard. The narcissistic object, "What one would like to be," remained alongside the sexual object. A further significant development ensued. The members developed a kind of conscience which kept whatch on their living up to or failing to live up to the ego-ideal; this involved many, often painful, modifications of behavior and sacrifice of older sources of pleasure in the pursuit of new ones, processes encouraged and aided by the leaders. That this compelling ego-ideal was narcissistic and not altruistic was evident in the group's constituting itself a strictly closed society, wishing to separate itself from all the other inmates and yet to dominate them. All the wishes for uniforms, the importance of whistles and badges, seemed to indicate a great wish to uplift the ego, partly by showing off the Group privileges and partly by limiting its membership to a carefully chosen few, thereby making it more desirable and more respected.

Narcissism predominated over libidinal fixation to the Leaders up to the intake of juniors. After this point, farreaching love for the leaders became obvious. With leaders and seniors for models and conscience, the newly admitted youngsters underwent much the same kind of development as their elders, trying to live up to the standards required of them. Their role was essentially one of passive, unquestioning obedience. To the seniors they were objects of activity, to be watched over, trained, and directed. The seniors' personal attitudes toward the new boys varied. Some six of them made "good friends" among them, though their "very good [best] friends" remained among fellow seniors. As noted earlier, some boys (Richard, Emil, Aaron, Marcus) acted as foci of friendships. Other seniors, though they guarded and trained juniors equally strictly, regarded the new entrants merely as serving to bring the number of members up to the required count of twenty.

The seniors who acted as "foci" seemed to be the kind that appear at the center in most youth groups and societies. The grouping round them showed that the degree of homosexual fixation was not the same in all of them, rather that attraction and antipathy were interpersonally variable. Only the four boys mentioned above were loved by all and they themselves varied in the intensity of libido issuing from them and directed toward them. Observation showed no evidence of heterosexual tendencies. Their attitude to the girls who wanted to exercise with them was one of rejection. This can be traced to their personal sexual overvaluation, partly in compensation for infantile castration (circumcision) and partly arising from ego estimation, fixation to a "big one" as ego-ideal as distinct from "the little ones." Only personal analyses could have revealed whether unconscious identification with the mother played any part in determining the homosexual object choice.

The requirements cited by Bernfeld (1922) for description of school groups would seem to have been met here, particularly in regard to "analysis of the factors determining the peculiar nature of members of a group." We have in part established "the connection of general group building factors with basic drives." But Bernfeld's schematic classification of school societies cannot be applied to our Group. School groups usually form among boys who share wishes that are denied realization by school or home, thus forming a personal world for its members in contrast with an environment that is against them. For the Group, the Home was not an object of aversion against which it directed its actions; it was what the Group worked for. This may have been an attempt to integrate the Home into the Group ego. Though conditioned by drives similar to those of other school groups, its social effects extended far beyond the closed circle of the members. The contradiction between the fantasied aim of the group and its real fulfillment, so characteristic of most school groups, is much less pronounced in our case. The activity of the Group, geared to the realization of its wishes and declared intentions, seems comparable only to those rare youth groups which evoke movements among the young and attain social significance by endeavoring to realize their aims. Although conditioned by similar basic drives, the social effect of youth groups depends on whether they form in a youthful milieu, like ours, or in a society of adults or with their cooperation. The social significance of youth groups requires more extensive research, and the case described here can only be regarded as an initial attempt at investigation.

9

Siegfried Bernfeld and "Jerubbaal": An Episode in the Jewish Youth Movement

AN EPISODE IN THE JEWISH YOUTH MOVEMENT*

Were it not for his association with Sigmund Freud and psychoanalysis, Dr. Siegfried Bernfeld's name would hardly be remembered nowadays. Yet it was he who, in 1918, caused a stir by sponsoring a new kind of Jewish Youth Movement which was intended to be autonomous and comprehensive, a challenge to the world of adults born out of the revolutionary mood of the last phase of the war. He also provided a tiny section of immigrants in Palestine with a blueprint for kibbutz-education shortly after the First World War. How did this become possible?

During the closing years of the First World War, Siegfried
Bernfeld became active in the Jewish Youth Movement in Vienna.
He had been one of the leading figures of the prewar youth
movement in Germany and Austria connected mainly with the circle
around Gustav Wyneken. He became converted to Zionism when
the influx of Jewish refugees from the Eastern parts of the Empire
(Galicia and Bukovina) revealed to him, as to many others, the
complicated nature of the "Jewish question." He got in touch with
youth leaders and intellectuals among these refugees who made a
great impression on him, he realized the potentialities of these
masses of youth who came from surroundings quite different from
those he had known in the West. These adolescents had been well
organized in their homeland but had already divided into parties
and factions, often in accordance with the Zionist affiliations of the
adults. Bernfeld concevied the idea of a large Jewish Youth Alliance
which, in spite of differences of opinion on social, religious and
other matters, should be united by the "idea of Youth". It should be
based on the autonomy of youth, allowed to live according to their
own existential requirements, as opposed to the adults with their
conventional political, social, economic and organizational prejudices. The first step in the attainment of this aim was the
convocation of a big Youth Rally in Vienna in May, 1918.

In our age when the holding of mass rallies of young people and
others has become a frequent occurrence, often for political
demonstrations and in the wake of political parties, it is difficult to
recall what a revolutionary event this first Jewish Youth Rally was
at that time. It was totally unique, and it was ventured in the midst of
a great war, in a country shaken by events and obviously facing
defeat. Bernfeld's ingenuity and the persuasive magic of his
personality succeeded in winning over all those concerned and in
overcoming the considerable obstacles. The rally took place in one
of the largest halls of Vienna, the *Grosse Musikvereinsaal* from the
18th to 20th May, 1918, and was completely dominated by Bernfeld,
its president. Bernfeld had also secured the cooperation of Martin
Buber, who delivered his famous speech "*Zion and die Jugend*"
(republished 1963). The hall was filled by an enthusiastic crowd,
although many of those who would have been interested could not

attend because they were in military service (the writer of these lines included). So the bulk of the audience consisted of youngsters below military age, to which were added, apart from girls, young men who for one reason or another had already been released from the army and others who were not physically fit for service, were on leave from the front or doing service in the metropolis. The large Zionist youth organization *Hashomer Hatzair* of Galicia (not to be confused with what was later called *Hashomer Hatzair* in Palestine, where it became a political party of Marxian denomination) formed a considerable part of the assembly. This group did not conform to Bernfeld's principles of freedom, advocating a stricter form of education and pleading especially for coercive Hebraization. One of the spectacular events of the Jugendtag was the inspired speech, delivered in fluent Hebrew, by the young Eliezer Rieger, at that time the acknowledged leader of the *Hashomer Hatzair*. Rieger (1896-1954) later became prominent in Palestine as one of the leading educators, headmaster of the model secondary school in Jerusalem and holder of a chair of education at the Hebrew University.

In spite of the disagreements voiced at the rally, it ended in a mood of solidarity and resulted in the establishment of a comprehensive organization, the *Verband der Juedischen Jugend Oesterreichs*, of which Bernfeld naturally became president. It was composed of the various organizations, which retained their independence, and had its headquarters at Obere Donaustrasse in the second district of Vienna (Leopoldstadt). The theses submitted by Bernfeld were accepted (Juedische Zeitung, nos. 20, 21, May 1918). The basis of the unity of youth was established in spite of the overt controversy, which had not been resolved, between those advocating the primacy of human values (which in their view would also ultimately promote nationalistic virtues) and those contending that, under the prevailing circumstances, youth had to subordinate all other considerations to the necessities of building a national entity and preparing for pioneer life in Palestine. Although the new large and powerful Association was part of an active Zionist movement, the official Zionist authorities looked with skepticism and even suspicion at the rebellious youth which proclaimed its autonomy and did not easily accept party discipline.

Bernfeld, however, felt that this work was not finished. In 1919 he published a book "The Jewish People and its Youth," followed in 1921 by "The Baumgarten Children's Home." These two publications had been preceded by *Jerubbaal*, a monthly of (not for) Jewish youth, edited by Bernfeld. It had been in circulation for one year only, 1918–1919, but among its steady or occasional contributors were a number of well-known authors, most of them Zionists, including: Victor Ch. Arlosoroff, Hugo Bergman, Adolf Boehm, Martin Buber, Eugen Hoeflich (now M.J. Ben Gavriel), Erwin Iohn (a Blau-Weiss member, later a high-ranking economist in Moscow), E. Elijahu Rapporport (later the cobbler of Beth Alpha), Schalom Adler-Rudel, Gerhard Scholem, Abraham Schwadron, Fritz Saxl (later of the Warburg Insitute) Monczi (now Mosche) Spitzer, Ludwig Strauss, Felix Weltsch, Robert Weltsch, and several more.

These publications suggest that there is a link still missing in the recorded history of the Zionist Youth Movement in Central Europe and that this link ought to be added to the historical accounts published earlier in the Year Book and Bulletin of the Leo Baeck Institute. (See Year Books IV and VI, 1959, 1961).

THE GERMAN YOUTH MOVEMENT OF GUSTAV WYNEKEN

Siegfried Bernfeld was born on May 7th, 1892, the son of a Viennese wholesale merchant. Tall and slim, precocious in his intellectual development, very keen on reading rather than on physical achievements, he concentrated early on the study of biology, and then on the study of social and educational psychology, a newly growing field. These preoccupations soon drew him to read Freud, that is to say, the then published first third of Freud's total work, and this work had a lasting influence on him throughout his life. Bernfeld died in San Francisco in 1953.

It was through the German monthly journal *Der Anfang* that Seigfried Bernfeld showed himself to be a follower of Gustav Wyneken (1875–1964), the founder and headmaster of the Freie Schulgemeinde Wickersdorf in Thuringia. At this coeducational boarding school Wyneken sought to create an environment in which adolescents could find and develop a style of living appropriate to their age rather than pursuing a prescribed course of studies and formal preparation for a profession. Wyneken thought that adolescents not only do not need to be taught and patronized by adult teachers, but that they ought to be free from the pressure of the conventional, disciplinary middle-class school. For young people to deveop imaginative thinking and those creative powers which the state of adolescence uniquely evokes, Wyneken hoped that Wickersdorf should be the place where youth could, by its own endeavors, discover and feel responsible for those values which only adolescents were suited to identify with and appreciate.

Wyneken's ideas were no doubt woolly, like much of the middle-class idealism of his time. While Bernfeld subscribed to the anti-authoritative aspect of Wyneken's message and to his rational and organizing approach to the problem, he proved his independence in his first contribution to *Der Anfang,* when he suggested the creation of "Archives" in which young people's contributions to culture, of the past and of the present, should be collected and made available for the scientific study of adolescence (1913). He, so to speak, accepted Wyneken's claim but tried to subject it to scrutiny. (Some years later, from 1920 to 1924, Bernfeld wrote and worked for a similar project which he called "Jewish Institute of Research into Adolescence and Education" and succeeded in publishing two volumes *Contributions to Research into Adolescence* in the Internationale Psychoanalytischer Verlag, Vienna).

Whether or not Bernfeld attended the famous Freideutsche youth gathering at the *Hoher Meissner* in 1913, I do not know. There Gustav Wyneken proclaimed his ideas and ideals, which were not generally approved. To this meeting "a cable had been sent by Blau-Weiss, then led by B.I.C. and K.Z.V. members" (Year Book IV, 1955). For a short while Bernfeld became Wyneken's mouthpiece in Vienna. When Wyneken attended a meeting there, he let himself be worshiped by a mixed group of German and Jewish youth.

The "youth movement" which Bernfeld had instigated in Austria resisted being drawn into the controversy between the still flourishing "german-liberal" and "Zionist students" organizations which, like the just emerging Blau-Weiss, were thought to be dependent on and influenced by the goals and values of adult society. Everything which seemed to be imitated or borrowed from adult society and organizations was felt to be repulsive and alien to the genuine feelings of adolescents. Suspicion and criticism of parental hypocrisy, partiularly of the "dancing-class" attitude and official "sexual morality," as well as of half-hearted nationalism, be it the German nationalism of the "assimilationists" or the superficial Jewish nationalism of the Zionists—all these and many more strong feelings, made this group cohesive, and vocal. The claim that the period of adolescence had a social function beyond that of just going to school must have been a challenge to the prevailing Jewish middle-class conventions.

That these ideals of *Jugendbewegung*, of which we shall hear more when we turn to *Jerubbaal*, could be understood and applied only be the few, had to be foreseen. Thus this group was suspected by its followers of aiming at an elite status, which the "lower ranks" resented, subsequently withholding their sustained enthusiasm and support.

The Wyneken Episode of the Jewish Youth Movement may be of little importance for the Jewish Historian, but its more remote effect on the Jewish community, itself having just become aware of the impact of Zionist nationalism, should not be underrated. The traditional religious formalism lost its meaning more and more for youth which had been conditioned by modern European ideas. The Zionist trend was more strongly represented in the Maccabee and Blau-Weiss movements, neither of which could actually commit themselves to the Youth Movement of Siegfried Bernfeld because of their close link with the adult Zionist organizations.

"THE WAR ORPHANS"

The seriousness of a new Jewish nationalism, which now began to penetrate the Jewish family and even the *Kultus Gemeinde* made itself felt in Central Europe during the early part of First World War and, as far as the intellectuals were concerned, it found expression in Martin Buber's monthly *Der Jude* (founded in 1916). Its first volume contains an article, "The War Orphans" by Siegfried Bernfeld, then twenty-four years old, which shows that meanwhile he had committed himself to the Jewish-national cause. In "The War Orphans" Bernfeld discussed with almost prophetic vision and not without realism the necessity for thinking and planning ahead the future of those Jewish children and adolescents who had been orphaned physically or psychologically, in consequence of the flight to the West of vast numbers of Austrian Jews from the Eastern provinces of the Hapsburg Monarchy, in face of the invading Imperial Russian armies, during 1914 and 1915. These children had either lost their parents or been separated from them. To think of them constructively was not a philanthropic or merely a welfare problem but, Bernfeld said, a national problem of the utmost importance. Was there not here the opportunity to provide these children, several hundred if not thousands of them (nobody knew how many there actually were) with an education and professional training which would not leave it to chance whether they would return to their semi-ghetto communities after the war, or become absorbed into the Jewish proletariat of the Leopoldstadt in Vienna, of Berlin, Frankfurt, or Brooklyn? Could one tolerate the fact that these children would be brought up in the pitiful orphanages which were all the *Kultusgemeinden* or the religious organizations could afford? Had not the time come to begin training them for a productive life in a progressive soceity? Why should they not grow up in an environment suitable for training in agriculture, artisanship, or in handling machines? What would their chances be if they became more and more involved with Western civilization and ambitions? Would these uprooted, lonely, aimless, and traumatized children ever again have a chance to learn how to contribute actively to the future Jewish cause? The loss of their parents had deprived them of their last living ties with the Jewish culture of the East. Moreover, there were no prototypes anywhere in the world for Jewish education, except the religious, fossilized *cheder*. Was not this a challenging occasion, an experiment of nature, which had to be met by a planned experiment in Jewish modern education? Could Jewish philanthropism, humanism, and nationalism not be brought into line and make a concerted effort now, when the tragedy was so fresh and calling for a remedy?

Bernfeld was realistic, if not scientifically minded enough, in merely outlining the problem and not proposing a detailed solution. Moreover, he must at that time already have been aware of, and unable to decide for himself against, the antagonism between the Hebrew-Zionist and Yiddish-Socialist factions within modern Jewish nationalism. Like every Jewish activist of that time he was convinced that whatever the future might bring after the war, one prediction could be made for these war orphans: conditions, political and economic, would have changed, should they ever return to their burned or ransacked homes. Therefore, the worst that could happen to them was their being absorbed into Western Jewry; the best, their becoming settlers in Palestine or, as could not be ruled out at that time, in new autonomous Jewish communities in the East. Much discussing and planning on these questions must have gone on in the coffee-houses of Vienna by those who had not yet been called up or were exempted from joining the army of the Austrian Monarchy.

Bernfeld was in a somewhat favorable position; his aesthenic build and tuberculous appearance had for some time saved him from active military service and he did military office work in Vienna, wearing the uniform of a private (or none at all). He was a young doctor of philosophy, quite capable of making a good research worker and of finding a place at a university. He was a compelling writer but still more fascinating as a lecturer; he could instill enthusiasm and belief rather than conviction of a final truth, of which he himself was doubtful.

JERUBBAAL

What Bernfeld needed were people who, by their understanding of the problem and their knowledge and capability for planning, could work with him. He was not, as he had been thought to be, a dreamer and talker. He was, in fact, a hard worker, but in cooperation with others he needed to have his terms respected. It was still wartime, and there was growing scarcity everywhere. The impact of thousands of Jewish refugees on the Jewish middle class and the growing competitiveness of the newcomers kindled resentment and still more fear of anti-Semitism as well as feelings of solidarity with the refugees, who could claim that by fleeing before the Russians they had proved their Austrian patriotism and their loyalty to Hapsburg. That must have been conducive to a more active Jewish nationalism, for the Austrian patriotism itself was already disintegrating. The question "What will happen to us?" became more urgent and was asked in the synagogues as well as by the Jewish soldiers in the army. Martin Buber had shown that in spite of wartime restrictions, Jewish thinkers, planners, and organizers could join together and pursue an active national policy in *Der Jude.*

But what would be the place of Jewish youth in that newly emerging Jewish nationalism? In March 1918, Siegfried Bernfeld published the first number of a monthly periodical dedicated to this problem, from R. Loewit Verlag, Vienna. No other word, embracing Jewish history and a programme for an active Jewish-national Youth Movement, could have expressed Bernfeld's ideas more aptly than that which he had chosen: *Jerubbaal.* It epitomized everything for which he was prepared to stand. It was taken from the biblical Book of Judges, where the story is told of Gideon, son of Joas, who together with ten other youths, revolted against their elders until these finally accepted humiliation and admitted their sins and failures. It was a story of the young, who did not just rebel but faced up to and acted against the hypocrisy, falsehood, and opportunism of their elders, who worshipped both Jahve and Baal. It was a revolt in which the elders had been given time for learning from the young and for admitting their failure, a victory of the young over the old not amounting to patricide but a victory free from guilt, a victory of true heroism!

But it was a dangerous emblem Bernfeld and those who supported him had chosen; one need hardly enlarge on it. The symbol expressed, as Bernfeld must have known, the idea that youth contains a revolutionary, even destructive, element which, if unleashed without the control of knowledge and experience, not to mention wisdom, can as readily destroy as create. Both Zionist nationalism and Yiddish Socialism of that time could turn in either direction, both were preparing but—it was still wartime—not yet calling for action. For that, there was as yet no basis. Herzl's booklet *Judenstaat* existed, but the Balfour Declaration was hardly born and almost unknown in Central Europe at war with the West. What the Yiddish Socialists had to offer was vague Marxist idealism, overshadowed by the uncertainty of the outcome of the Bolshevik revoltion, then just a few months old.

Still, in few places of the Jewish world of that time had a group of thinking and educated people, politically powerless, economically weak and not believing in religious ceremonial and tradition, been feeling and planning so seriously for a Jewish national future as had the groups behind *Der Jude* and *Jerubbaal*. But while the former spoke for a section of the Central European Zionist intelligentsia, the latter had to reach an audience and create an avant garde—the Jewish Youth Movement—which then scarcely existed. Its representatives were either in uniform or inaccessible to Bernfeld's ideas and to the mission which he tried to make them accept and act upon.

The task which Bernfeld set himself in *Jerubbaal* was different from the ideas developed by Gustav Wyneken in his book *School and Youth Culture* (1913). Wyneken, unaware of the function of working-class youth in economic life, had addressed himself exclusively to the German middle-class youths who spent eight years at school and had their lives conditioned there according to the needs of that class. Bernfeld, in contrast, had to take into account a much wider spectrum of youthful ideologies and aspirations, particularly those labeled *Posle Zion* and *Hashomer Hatzair*. Jewish East and West had for the first time come into direct physical contact during the war and a real problem had emerged, which formerly could only be imagined. Hence, the literary platform for the Jewish Youth Movement had to be a wide and a controversial one.

The life of *Jerubbaal* was brief, for reasons that are easy to understand. The difficulties Bernfeld and his writers in *Jerubbaal* had in arousing a response to the idea of an autonomous youth movement had to be expected; the material and ideational dependence of youth on adult society could certainly not be changed at short notice, if at all. More important, political events began to overtake Bernfeld's preparatory and educational work. The time had come—or was felt to have come—for action in building Jewish nationalism, and there was little sympathy for those fostering somewhat separatist ideals. To understand this conflict, one must consider the general political scene in Central Europe during the crucial year 1918. There was general revolutionary upheaval. The prospect of a Jewish national home in Palestine had suddenly become brighter than ever before. The British government had issued the Balfour Declaration, and competing with it, again on paper, the German government, on behalf of its Turkish ally, had made some kind of promise to the Jews too. On the other hand, the Yiddishists and Socialists in Vienna and Berlin counted on Jewish autonomy in the East, in the belief that socialists there would adopt a favorable attitude toward a Jewish working-class and its national aspirations.

But how would the Jews, particularly the young ones, become prepared for the new Jewish communities of the future? The immediate aim was twofold: turning Jewish youth away from the idea that they had to follow in their parents' footsteps and become traders, doctors, tailors or cobblers, instead of learning to handle machines and tractors; and providing training and achieving efficiency in productive occupations. Where were the workshops, factories, farms where young Jews could be trained? Where were the teachers who would instruct the new generation and imbue them with modern Jewish spirit? Where would the transformation of the Galuth-Jew into the National Jew take place? It was at this time that the Association for the Welfare of Jewish Youth and the *Paedagogium*, the training college for Jewish teachers, took shape in Vienna—largely at the office in the Obere Donaustrasse in the Leopoldstadt. The *Paedagogium*, an interesting and novel experiment, had as its object the training of modern teachers for Jewish subjects who would combine a thorough knowledge of Judaism in all its aspects with a modern Bernfeld-inspired approach to education and to youth in general. It was the brainchild of Siegfried Bernfeld who, in this matter as in others, collaborated closely with

. men like Abraham Sonne and Adolf Bohm. Among the teachers of the *Paedagogium* were Dr. Aptowitzer (Talmud), chief Rabbi Dr. Z.P. Chajes (Bible), Zwi Dizendruck (philosophy of religion), Salo Baron (Jewish history), and many others who later occupied important positions elsewhere. There were several courses in Hebrew and one of Bernfeld's most devoted pupils, Greta Obernik (later in Palestine), taught child psychology. Although the *Paedagogium*, like many creations of the revolutionary enthusiasm of those years, had only a short span of life, and although most of its teachers dispersed after 1921 and continued their work elsewhere (primarily in Palestine and the United States), its direct or indirect educational influence is still felt in some places throughout the Jewish world of today.

By the end of October 1918, the Austro-Hungarian monarchy finally dissolved, and the war came to its end. In Vienna the Jewish National Council was formed with Bernfeld as one of its secretaries. For some time this council was the only active, organized authority which could speak for the Jews. During the chaos, attendant upon the Emperor's abdication and the emergence of new states, the Jewish National Council acted for a day or two as a kind of public authority in the Leopoldstadt, with Bernfeld as Commandant of the improvised Jewish National Guard, consisting mainly of soldiers returning from the front. It sounds like a joke but it was true. Afraid of possible excesses of the demoralized masses of the disintegrating Empire, Bernfeld took the initiative in defending the Leopoldstadt with its densely populated ghetto of mainly Galician origin. A few resolute Jews with blue-white armlets and rifles had been looking after the law, taking care of food supplies and asserting security and public authority in the name of the Jewish National Council.

A periodical was for Bernfeld more than a literary mouth-piece. It was to be a nucleus around which to rally people who were determined to devote themselves to a cause. *Jerubbaal* was a battle-cry and Bernfeld wanted to make it the name for a group of people identifying themselves with Gideon's brave followers. With this end in mind, he organized his closest friends in a kind of monastic secret order called the "Order Jerubbaal" (Orden Jerubbaal, abbreviated O.J.). Those who were attached to this center but were not called upon to take upon themselves such strict commitments, were called "Circle Jerubbaal" (Kreis Jerubbaal, K.J.). A regular circular letter conveyed to all concerned information on relevant events, personal matters, problems of education and Zionist work, mostly in opposition to the official Zionist party. Both the "Order" and the "Circle" ceased to exist after some time, when Bernfeld himself assumed other responsibilities. Conditions had changed radically. When all were preoccupied with urgent personal and public affairs and many members of Bernfeld's circle left Vienna, *Jerubbaal* could find neither collaborators nor enough subscribers. Having no financial backing, it had to discontinue publication.

THE JEWISH PEOPLE AND ITS YOUTH

As mentioned above, in 1919 Siegfried Bernfeld published a book on Jewish education. In it he envisioned an educational system which embraced every aspect of life from birth to maturity. Nobody would have expected Bernfeld to speak for what was then being hotly discussed as "school reform." For Bernfeld was not a reformer but a man who thought that if one knew enough of the natural and social history of the state of being young, and of the laws of growth and development, and if one prepared the best of men and women to live with the young, only the best could result. Moreover, there was nothing left of Jewish education which deserved reformation. One could only start form rock-bottom and, by doing so, either think anew or adopt and imitate the pattern of the hosts, e.g. a *Gymnasium* (as was done with the Chojes Gymnasium in Vienna). Bernfeld believed the best and most modern type of education would be just good enough for an emerging nation's young generation. If he were alive today, he would be delighted with the educational achievements of some of the kibbutzim, but he would turn away in horror from the copies of what he considered to be the worst of Western education.

Bernfeld's position is elucidated by the persons to whom he dedicated his book, the most original and creative educators of his time. First came Dr. Maria Montessori, the Italian physician, whose system of "self-education" of the younger child was little known and often hotly contested by the German Froebel kindergarten teachers. Nowadays we take Montessori for granted and, apart from some details, her method is not disputed. The 'do-it-yourself' method has become the most appropriate and rewarding principle or practice in modern education and child upbringing.

The second person to whom the book was dedicated was Bethold Otto. He was a rather obscure school teacher in Berlin, who by his own intuition and unshakable trust in children of school age, had transformed his elementary school into a place of learning, free from timetables and enforced discipline and full of joy and scholastic brilliance. One ought to know about the five contemporaries of Bernfeld, to whom his book was dedicated, because they represent educational realities and not the phantasms which the traditionalists and timid reformers saw in them and in Bernfeld.

The third name was Gustav Wyneken. Bernfeld had learned from Wyneken that a nation's youth will never be genuinely youthful, which of course includes being rebellious and noisy at times, as long as adult society does not respect and give way to the propensities, creative as well as explosive, which are innate in the adolescent state. Wyneken had shown that traditional schooling leads to exploitation and exhaustion of the receptive and productive qualities of the adolescent. Going beyond Wyneken, Bernfeld had learned from his socialist friends that most of that is equally true, often still more so, of the juvenile apprentice in the workshop, in the factory and in any form of employment or training. Wyneken was for Bernfeld the man who respected youth without reservation and taught his teachers at Wickersdorf to let themselves be carried along by young people's enthusiasm and creativity. It was Bernfeld's young follower Erwin Kohn (then still a strong Zionist) who pointed out the impracticability of "adolescence for adolescents" on the ground of the interwovenness of adult economic organization with the acquisition of skills during adolescence. Erwin Kohn insisted that the machine age sets limits on the autonomous status of adolescence which Wyneken had so much at heart.

The fourth contemporary from whom Bernfeld drew his ideas was Granville Stanley Hall, the American professor of psychology. Hall pioneered research into adolescence and published a book called

Adolescence in two encyclopaedic volumes (1924). The prominent place Bernfeld accorded G.S. Hall in his book indicates that he did not accept Wyneken's conception unreservedly and wanted it scientifically tested. But before that could be ahieved, Bernfeld insisted, the attitude to adolescence, his field of observation, had first to be changed so that adolescents reveal more of themselves than they can under the conditions imposed on them by adult society. He saw Jewish national education as an integrated whole, believing that how to teach adolescents cannot be learned at colleges, it has to be experienced in a mutual, interchangeable relation. To Erwin Kohn's objections Bernfeld retorted that young men and women would not only have to learn how to handle machines, tools, plants, or animals but would also have to learn how to care about them.

The fifth who must be mentioned as a decisive influence on Bernfeld was Sigmund Freud, the then still little recognized founder of an all-embracing psychology of man. That Bernfeld should extol Freud does not need explaining, though it was not yet customary at that time. It was not the medical aspect of psychoanalysis, but the preventive one that Bernfeld made use of. The former, based on psychopathology, is understood as referring to therapy or healing, while prevention demands positive measures, so that illness and the necessity for healing will not arise. But it is not as simple as that, if one understands and applies Freud's psychology to education. Bernfeld had learned from Freud, though Freud had never said this explicitly, as I try to do here, that psychopathological development during childhood and infancy is—within limits, of course—normal, though in no way harmless or negligible. It is difficult to convey the meaning of that statement comprehensively. What is meant can be compared with the infectious diseases of childhood; they too are harmless and normal, and we take them for granted; but we also know that measles or mumps can lead to disastrous complications from the child's point of view. Still, we welcome them, because they bring about a considerable degree of immunity for later life. While the normal psychopathology of childhood and adolescence is not the same, it is not too different. Therefore, Bernfeld's conception of education covered this aspect of psychopathology, and prevention meant to him reacting to and providing for the child's normal psychopathology in the right and not in the wrong way. In this attitude Bernfeld was ans till is, far ahead of the overall conception of "preventive" education, as it was and still is generally understood. His conception can be called heroic, and it is that which makes his book appear so utopian.

Bernfeld pictured in some detail how education has to be organized in order to offer the child and adolescent the best of conditions for growth and health. He did not think of fathers and mothers, sons and daughters, but of wise men and great women to whom the child and his adult helpers could look up. To develop a sense of self-reliance in earliest childhood, the mother herself has to be provided with everything, so that she can dedicade herself to her children: then comes the "children's house" which is locally but not emotionally segregated from the parental community. At school the child lives in an environment which gives full scope for "self-education" in small communities. Education means living in an environment completely adjusted to the young who one day will want to be fully adult themselves. The pace of development and of reaching adulthood will be controlled by the child's innate capabilities, not prescribed by adult society. It was a utopian picture of education, a daydream, but it did not contradict reality, for there was as yet no Jewish national education which Bernfeld could have contradicted.

THE BAUMGARTEN CHILDREN'S HOME

On October 15, 1919, The Baumgarten Children's Home for Jewish orphans was opened and Siegfried Bernfeld was appointed its full-time, "living-in" director; his wife, Dr. Anne Bernfeld, was the home's part-time physician. After the Baumgarten experiment collapsed, Bernfeld's book describing the whole enterprise and the underlying idea, was published in 1921. The assignment which Bernfeld had accepted was the outcome of his article on "The War Orphans," published in *Der Jude*, 1916. The money was provided by the American Joint Distribution Committee.

Because I took part in the Baumgarten experiment, just by chance and without premeditation, and, as Bernfeld stated in his book, after some time played a leading part in its running, I may be permitted here to describe briefly how this came to be the case.

I first read of Bernfeld, when, in May 1918, as an Austrian soldier I was transferred from the army in the Ukraine to that on the Piave in Italy; when walking in Vienna from the Nordbahnhof to the Sudbahnhof I stopped at R. Loewit's bookshop in the Rothenturmstrasse, and bought *Jerubbaal*. From about 1913 on, I had been a member of the Blau-Weiss and together with Franz Kahn, later well-known as a Zionist organizer, I had founded the Blau-Weiss in Pilzen, now Czechoslovakia. The idea of Wyneken's *Jugendbewegung* was known to me but was rather outside my interests. I may mention that Zionism was at that time something of a provocation to my family, who lived in what has become known as Sudentenland (the German-speaking part of Bohemia). It was feared that Zionism might arouse still more anti-Semitism among those notorious pan-German nationalists. I was therefore nicknamed at home as "the *Zionmist*" (meaning Zion and dung). Military service in the Austrian army, however, had reinforced my ideals, for as a Jew one had to prove that one was not a coward and had to face up to more danger than was expected of the average man. The war over, most of us thought of emigrating to Palestine and that was a further threat, at first, to our families. I went to Vienna to start studying veterinarian surgery in order to become a veterinarian in Palestine. So it came about that I could listen to Bernfeld, who often spoke to us on the roof terrace of the Eugenie Schwarzwald school in Vienna. I was very active in the Blau-Weiss of Vienna, and in September 1919 Bernfeld approached me personally for the first time. He said that a home for Jewish war orphans would be opened soon and asked whether I would give up one day (he mentioned the fifteenth of October) to come and prepare some cages for rabbits and chickens, so that the children could learn to look after them.

I appeared at the bleak Baumgarten former military hospital barracks early on that day, October 15th, 1919. I brought some wire netting, nails, and a hammer but nowhere could I get the necessary wooden boxes. I made myself useful by joining a considerable number of voluntary helpers who were preparing the home for the expected two to three hundred children and youths. In charge of the preparations was Mrs. Patak, a lady well known in Jewish welfare work and an ardent Zionist (who, in spite of her age was, very much later, to carry out useful welfare work in the concentration camp of Theresienstadt). In the huge "dining room" the ladies nailed oilcloth on the rough tables, taken over from the military. I found they were doing it wrong; they merely covered the tops of the tables and did not turn the cloth under the edges and nail it from below. I showed them how it should be done. (Two weeks later, the room smelt foul and we found that the children had been playing games on those tables which had been covered in the wrong way. They had squeezed beans and lentils under the cloth toward the middle of the table, those children winning whose beans first reached the center!)

The children were marched in later in the afternoon together with their guardians from the various orphanages. Among them there were about ten deaf-and-dumb boys, some quite big. Nobody knew how to manage them. They started ransacking the store room, where they stuffed their mouths with raw food. Bernfeld asked me to help in getting the deaf-and-dumb boys out of the way, and I did so with the aid of a football. So it came about that I settled at Baumgarten as a voluntary helper, and a fortnight later I knew that I should never return to the dissection of my horse at the veterinary school.

In his book, Bernfeld describes the events which led to some of the successes and to some of the disasters of the Baumgarten experiment. There were two hundred and forty children, about forty under five, a similar number over fourteen, the rest of the usual school age. These were taught in classrooms by enthusiastic Jewish teachers, some of them borrowed from Viennese schools and outstandingly experienced and active in the movement for "school reform." Their enthusiasm was met by most of the children who proved as hungry for knowledge as they were hungry for food. Naturally, the children had no aim other than getting out of the home as soon as possible; in fact, two months later, over one hundred had left for Denmark and Holland, where they were invited as guests by Jewish families. Some of them returned to the home later, their middle-class ideals reinforced and almost inaccessible to the ideals we wanted to make them aware of, i.e., Jewish national feeling, preparing for work and for Palestine. The children were, as Bernfeld described so vividly, bewildered by the helpers' attitude; in the orphanages they were used to being told what to do and what not to do, and also to being punished or favored as the adult should decide or wish. Bernfeld frequently called them to a kind of parliamentary session, facing them all in one room, including even the smallest. He had an impact on the adolescents, some of them students of the *Paedagogium.* They became enthusiastic themselves and formed groups round some of the teachers and helpers. However there were constantly disturbing outbreaks of some kind of violence, against other children, against furniture and dining-room utensils, books and windows. The sanitary provisions as well as the habits of the children were deficient or lax, partly because of the absence of fear of corporal punishment. Officially, all offences had to be dealt with in a "court-meeting" where Bernfeld presided and guided the jury of older children. The punishment proposed by them, even for petty offenses, was usually quite out of proportion. Much improvement was noticed some time after the 'Histadruth' of the 12-14 year old boys had been formed, a type of "police force" who submitted to a kind of boy-scout discipline (Hoffer, 1922; Chapter 8). We all felt helpless with a few very disturbed children, psychopaths or perhaps brain-damaged; we had to leave them to the harsh disciplinary treatment handed out by the stronger boys. The deaf-and-dumb had long since gone to an appropriate home, but the emotionally deaf children still posed a major problem. Still, the community ideals started to work and some consolidation was noticeable after two months. It need hardly be said that the stability and reliability of the communities now forming was dependent on stability of leadership. Unfortunately, catastrophes were interfering with that. One befell first Bernfeld's own family and then himself near the end of the year 1919, just three months after the opening. In November Bernfeld's four-year-old daughter developed a "running ear"; she had fallen ill from active tuberculosis. Her mother went with her to Switzerland. I later found out that the room in which Bernfeld's two children had slept was the former postmortem room of the barrack for tuberculous soldiers. In December Bernfeld himself fell ill and remained so for many months, suffering from a febrile intestinal disease, probably tuberculous too. When he had recovered in the summer of 1920, Martin Buber invited him to Heppenheim an der Bergstrasse to stay with him and be his private secretary and assistant editor of *Der Jude*. Thus, after three months, Baumgarten was without Bernfeld, its founder and leader. No successor was ever appointed and, in fact, Gerhard Fuchs and I acted as if we were in charge; we were both voluntary helpers but were recognized by the official administrative committee, which we never faced, except for Mrs. Patak. We carried on on the understanding that we needed each other but did not really like each other.

By that time, with only one-hundred twenty children to live with, conditions were fairly normal, insofar as there were no unusual mishaps. The idea that we, the adults, did not want to receive or to give, but would like to live together and prepare for a life as Jews, with a growing strong accent on Palestine, took hold slowly but firmly. For a visitor and outsider all this was hardly noticeable, but one effect could not be missed. Everybody who met these children after the first two or three months and was informed enough to compare them with children from traditional orphanages, agreed that these were not "institution children," not even the smallest ones, who really had never known a family life, as the older ones had. That was the first important result of the workers' attitude to which the children could respond. Various other-steps in different directions, described by Bernfeld in his book, had also been taken.

What was the outcome of the experiment? In fact those who had come to Baumgarten with Bernfeld, including all the teachers, left the home on 15th April, 1920 and parted from the children. It was not possible to carry on without self-sacrifice beyond our intentions. Bernfeld gave an account of the reasons, as he and we felt and saw them. Throughout the six months of the Bernfeld Baumgarten there was an unending battle between the "administration" and the educational staff. Today I would say it was the fault of neither side but the misalliance ought never to have happened. The two sides had started from opposing viewpoints and there was a mutual deafness which made communication and understanding impossible.

Though on the surface we managed to cooperate, the children themselves sensed the gap and—naturally, we say today—took sides.

Since it has not been stated by Bernfeld in detail, I will describe the final explosion here. Passover was approaching, and the feast was very important for all of us and an emotional experience of the first order for the children. Most of them, particularly the more cooperative of the girls, had grown rather sentimental in respect of Bernfeld's ideals and devoted to him as a person, though he had not been present for more than three months. Without any forewarning from the 'administration' it became clear on the afternoon before the Seder, that an American mission of the Joint Distribution Committee would visit the home and take part. So far, so good; but we all resented the manner in which the home was prepared for the occasion, the private lockers of the children inspected and an impression given of our daily life which was quite untrue. We would have understood had we been asked to cooperate, but our consent was taken for granted. A similar situation had occurred soon after Benfeld had fallen ill, when the Chief Rabbi of Vienna, Dr. Chajes, visited the home. He was understanding and communicative enough, so I could tell him not to take the cleanliness and the white towels and flowers too seriously. I knew he understood. But this time the boys of the "Histadruth" became bewildered. They became abusive to the "administrator," a somewhat frightened official, who started an argument with the boys instead of asking us to help him. The boys proclaimed open resistance and made preparations for burning the dining room. They resented the difference in the food that was being prepared in the kitchen, and had heard rumors of bottles of genuine wine for the guests. The girls were heartbroken, their Seder in jeopardy and they themselves unable to pacify or convince the boys. Finally we persuaded the "administrator" to fill our rucksacks with food and we departed with the "Histadruth," just before the Seder, into the Vienna woods. We slept through a rather cold night there, watching the sunrise from a mountaintop. That was all we could do, and we took leave of the children and Baumgarten soon after.

I should perhaps mention that, as far as possible, we kept contact with the children for some time, and I know that quite a number of them continued to strive in the direction we had wished. Some of them went to Palestine, a few to Russia and the rest must have become absorbed in Vienna or joined relatives elsewhere, particularly in the United States.

After the Baumgarten experiment Bernfeld never returned as a youth leader but through the Jewish Institute for Research into Adolescence and for Education, which he had set up, he tried to infuse modern ideas into the thinking of Jewish teachers and educators. Twice he organized summer schools for Jewish teachers, which were attended by participants coming from Poland, Lithuania, Latvia and Palestine. For a short while in 1920, like almost all the Zionist members of his circle at that time, Berfeld contemplated immediate emigration to Palestine where, he hoped, a suitable field would be offered to him for the execution of the ideas which he pursued with almost missionary zeal. He suggested that the embryonic University in Jerusalem should establish a research institute for education and child psychology and appoint him as its head. He even tried to enlist the support of Dr. Albert Einstein for such a plan, which remained utopian like so many of Bernfeld's ideas. A letter Bernfeld wrote him about this matter on 15th March, 1921, is still in the possession of Robert Weltsch.

As it was, in the early twenties the worldwide Chaluz Movement had started vigorously to take over the leadership of Zionist youth, especially in Eastern Europe whose direct ties with Vienna had been loosened with the emergence of the new independent states. In the main it was in the Emek Yesre'el that Bernfeld's ideas came to life again and were put into practice in the Kibbutz education of the early twenties. Unknown in Israel today, he may still be considered one of the architects of a blueprint for that education, which has made its name throughout the civilized world.

10

Children's Fantasy Play and Its Relation to Poetic Creativity

It is essential that any consideration of play and play theories should take account of the connection between psychic manifestations in play and those particular experiences we believe we see in aesthetic enjoyment or in artistically creative activity. The speculative, if by no means unfruitful, methods hitherto employed (most closely linked with the name of Konrad Lange in the more recent play literature) must of course give way today to those more exact methods that correspond better to the current propositions of psychological science. We have taken the psychoanalytic method as one of these approaches into the inventory of well-known methods of youth research and must therefore give it central place in the present work. Since apart from its usefulness to us in obtaining and treating data, as will be shown later, it has already been used with much success, first by Freud (1907) and later by Rank (1907, 1912) in a field of research closely allied to ours, the utilization of these results alone must compel one to maintain the direction of research chosen by these authors.

Naturally the significance of psychoanalytic methods and theroy for the treatment of themes hirtherto reserved for the literary historian and critic cannot be the task of this work. Perhaps the communication of our data and some results which we present can serve as an example of how fruitful the methods used by us in youth research can be.

INTRODUCTION

In the present work *fantasy play* is to be understood as play that exhibits the following characteristics: It presupposes the participation of a group of children, it is many times repeated and its content is the presentation and elaboration of a day dream or a fantasy. The children themselves call it a game. The presentation of the fantasies is undertaken exclusively with the aid of speech; the physical activities otherwise characteristic of children's play, including the use of inanimate objects, are missing. This affords an important distinction between the form of play we are describing here and what we are accustomed to seeing in illlusory games. Though here too, we are right in describing the participation of fantasy as characteristic, the absence of activities supported by objects which arouse or make illusions possible, allows a true uniqueness to appear in our form of play. At present we still lack insight into the dynamics and economics of these two types of play, which do not seem to be distinguished in the literature. Hence, we shall limit ourselves to the division that our observation forces upon us. For this, *the absence of activity* is a decisive distinguishing characteristic.

This work is based on a young adult student's, Raimund R.'s, memories of play, written down by him and commented on by word of mouth a few weeks later. The recording of these oral elucidations required six sessions of one hour each. Shortly afterward Raimund submitted himself to psychoanalytic treatment for didactic reasons.

Only because of this did it become possible to attain deeper insight into the play. I am greatly indebted to Dr. Hermann Nunberg for the various communications he passed on to me about this analysis, naturally with Raimund's knowledge and consent. These broadened the data enough to make a thorough discussion possible.

The obtaining of data thus comprised three phases, which will be briefly detailed here because they have proved valuable as methods:

1. *Autobiographical presentation of data.* In this case, this technique provided, so to speak, the only document, often a most valuable illustration of the later oral statements.

2. *The question and answer method.* This interview method, arrived at for use here, needs considerable justification. The method as used by us is a combination of the research methods employed by Stern and by Freud (1909) in the treatment of young patients. Stern showed how to prevent any avoidable suggestion from the living or inanimate environment, from the preparation of the experiment, or from the play of words, while Freud taught us how to rectify, minimize or get rid of whatever unavoidable incidental influence or distortion might still remain. In the concrete, the making of a statement looks something like this: the research-subject, turned away from the observer in a resting or seated position, is asked to repeat every detail of the game. The account is written down verbatim, together with all the questions the observer (who is also the writer) may have interposed. The suitability of this or that question can be assessed later by means of the shorthand notes. The questions belong to the total presentation. Since the sessions are usually repeated after a day's interval, the questions can be well prepared. This preparation may seem superfluous to the trained analyst, but it must be remembered that the task of the experiment is to obtain a great deal of material in the shortest possible time. Its working up and significance will only be known to the research subject at earliest on publication. The observer thus endeavors to obtain a quantity of manifest data by many questions.

3. *Psychoanalysis.* This is certainly the most informative and reliable method.

After Raimund R. had related his material in all three of the methods cited, the consistency of his perceptions could not be doubted. Still, investigation of the content of a game naturally cannot be based on the statements of a single player, even if he is the leader of the game, and it was a great advantage when I had the opportunity to listen to the printer Josef G., now 26 years of age, who as a boy had participated with Raimund in the game.

To prevent the danger of premature generalization from a single instance, I have considered several other sources, including:

1. Two sisters' memories of play, told me by the younger one. These included an account of a fantasy game.
2. The autobiographical book by the dancer Grete Wiesenthal, *The Ascent* (Berlin: [*Der Aufstieg*] 1919), which related a quantity of valuable memories directly connected with our theme. These were further elaborated by some oral communications from Frau Martha Liebl-Wiesenthal.
3. Six accounts of games culled from ten accounts submitted by readers of the "Korrespondenzblattes des juedischen Institute fuer Jugendforschung und Erziehung" (No. 10) in response to one of my edited questions.

It was already emphasized in the beginning that the psychoanalytic method came to be used almost exclusively in the present work. It seems necessary to give briefly the grounds for the way in which this method has been presented here. The relation of German youth study and pedagogic research to psychoanalysis forces one to use here, rather than only in special cases, an otherwise no longer necessary way of presentation. Hence we are obliged to describe things already known in detail in order to make the sphere of youth research as viewed psychoanalytically, accessible to a wider audience. In the course of this effort, much that would be of particular interest to an analyst will have to be omitted or merely indicated.

ELABORATION AND CHANGES IN A YOUTHFUL SHARED FANTASY

Raimund is a pupil in the fourth class of the Volksschule (elementary school), 9½ years old, the only child of shopkeepers in a provincial town in Austria. One Sunday, during a walk with his parents, he saw a goat harnessed to a cart for the first time in his life. This belonged to the son of a local manufacturer. Raimund's extremely lively interest in this cart induced the father to discuss its purchase with the mother. For the present Raimund must settle for a less than binding promise; nevertheless, from this walk he took home with him some clover which he had picked for the he-goat at his father's bidding.

Next day Raimund told his fellow-pupil Josef G. all about the goat and in the afternoon discussed with him in his home ("because it was quiestest there") all the details connected with the goatcart. The repetition of thie conversation became "the he-goat game." Josef, at 10½ a year older than Raimund, the son of a day-laborer, was mostly at home all day long with his younger sister Paula (8½), while his elder brother, an apprentice, and his parents were at work.

Meetings now took place in Josef's home as often as he did not have to take a meal to his parents at their place of work (about three times a week). At first only the two boys took part in the goat game. Sometimes the game began with Raimund's question "What shall we do with the goat?" then followed the story, at first only Raimund's. (Copy from memoranda): "First we fetch him, you hold him by the halter, I sit on the box and brake [the ride includes a street going downhill]. Then we open the house door, lead him into the backyard, take off his harness like this [here follows a detailed description of every handhold in the unharnessing], then you lead him into the stable, hand up the harness and feed him" [the place for this was exactly indicated].

Then followed detailed remarks about the "outing." It is decided who shall sit on the box and drive, crack the whip and brake, and who will sit in the seat of honor. The feeding and cleaning of the stall is discussed, also the care of the harness. All child friends will be tested as to their worthiness to be "taken for a drive" (naturally only in conversation between the boys). Cracking of the whip—a favorite game of the coachman—is discussed.

In this way the two boys met for their "goat game" for three or four weeks, Raimund mostly being the only speaker. Sometimes Josef repeated parts of the story, obviously to show "how well he already can" (Raimund's words). After this time a small change came about. The chosen site of activity (where the story was played) was no longer the house of Raimund's father but became instead that of his grandmother which was not far from Josef' home. Josef, who now told the story more often, proposed to milk the goat in order to make cheese from the milk. Now Josef's sister was also brought into the game. She was allowed to listen and, as a co-player, was admitted to the content of the game. In the boys' stories she milked the goat and did part of the work of "cheese-making."One of the boys must always sleep in the stable. The dung, milk, and cheese were to be sold, and finally the undertaking of commissions for the shop people of the locality was discussed in great detail. In this way the game was repeated for two months. What changes, if any, it underwent during this time cannot be exactly determined.

In the dissection and analytic working-out of the play recounted above, we will turn first to the content of the game. The particular *form* of this play will only be discussed in the second part of the work.

Raimund's memories were so vivid that even his first description would have made the above reconstruction possible. Two phases in the game emerge clearly. The first phase is characterized by having two persons of the same sex and the same class at school as players, the story being mainly told in terms of "we" ("we do this and that"); there is no division of roles but there is an exchange of them. All the details are copies from reality; they are verbal reproductions of visual pictures. The combination of house-yard-stable (taken from reality) with the goat-cart (which had also been seen) are true to nature. The fantasy becomes a matter of drawing analogies based on experience. The boys had often had to do with horse- and ox-teams, and every single detail of the fantasies could be traced back to an earlier experience. Only the successful combination could be designated as original, because this was not based on any previous experience. Hence we can describe this process accurately as fantasy formation and not as reproduction. Its meaning is entirely clear: the fantasies are anticipations of the actual fulfillment of a wish and a promise. This phase of the game is a wish-fulfillment and shows no differences between conscious and unconscious fantasies, as in the children's dreams described by Freud. For the present this blending of conscious and unconscious fantasies is to be seen as characteristic of the first phase of play.

The change that the game underwent after three to four weeks, which gives us occasion to speak of a second phase, is, in the first instance, spatial. The whole inventory, he-goat and carriage, is now transposed to the garden of Raimund's grandmother. The good stable in Raimund's father's house is exchanged for a tumble-down garden shed, in which apparently there was room only for the goat and not for the cart. The entrance to the garden was also not wide enough. Nevertheless, the game was based on this place. Although earlier both the boys had often played in R.'s grandmother's garden, these experiences were ignored. Along with this neglect of spatial conditions, further facts come to notice: the milking of the goat is allocated to Paula, Josef's sister, (who thereby became a partner in the game), and the milk is distributed like a gift, to Raimund's and Josef's parents ("to the mother," as the reconstruction has it.). Milk is also sold and made into cheese. The cheese-making is again best explained by Josef. The proceeds from the sale of milk and cheese would be reckoned up. The packing of the cheese, which was bar-shaped, was explained by Josef. Raimund spoke about the sale of dung and the commissions and Paula also had something to say. The division of roles is now complete. Whereas in the first phase of play (in which, for Raimund, endopsychic images of movement and their transcription obviously played a part), every activity was most precisely described, in the second phase the description omits important details. This phase is govered by unrealistic, even absurd conceptions, like quantities of milk obtained from the milking of the he-goat. In contrast to phase 1, which was true to reality, phase 2 must be designated as estranged from reality.

In addition to these features characteristic of the content of the whole game, yet another occurs to us. The description of individual performances in phase 1 of the game (driving out, acting as coachman, cleaning, etc.) is logically well founded, includes no contradiction, and acknowledges causality. Phase 2, on the other hand is quite different. The fantasies connected with the milk business are in part derived from Raimund's and in part from Josef's sphere of experience but in part are just errors (like the belief that the he-goat would give milk). The fantasies were presented in the story without regard to contradictions and neglecting all spatial conditions and causal connections. This description concerned not only the environment but the players themselves; thus, for instance, Raimund drinks milk in the game though he never in fact liked drinking milk.

This change in the content of the game *while the form of play was retained*—the second phase also consisted only of speaking— unlikely as it may seem, should naturally become understandable in terms of its psychic bases. The statements of Raimund and Josef about the alteration of the content of the game were negative; indeed, the author nearly settled for a fragmentary explanation of the game. Then Raimund's analysis began, and a more fear-reaching explanation was to be hoped for. Thus, following the statement and question methods, the psychoanalytic is not only another but appears to be the best available method to supply additional contents of the game and their deeper meaning.

The game with the he-goat was apparently told several times during the course of the analysis. Raimund directed his attention, aroused by my earlier questions, to that point which had already interested me in the recording, the transition from the first to the second phase of play. He asked himself, "Why had the game changed at all?" The game derived from the first encounter with the he-goat and the attainment of the father's promise. Raimund was used to any promise being kept; on the other hand it was easy for him to create for himself in fantasy a substitute for external refusal. The fantasies about the he-goat have doubtless become an-ticipations of the actual wish-fulfillment. R. knew very well that the fulfillment of the wish finally depended on his father, he believed firmly in the promise, had picked clover at his father's bidding, and was thus prepared for realistic activity. Thus the anticipatory fantasies carried the stamp of true reality-testing, which indeed is characteristic of children of this age and social class (Buhler [1921] claims that other relationships can be observed in children of the proletariat). Although the adaptation to reality thinking (cf. Ferenczi [1916]) may be acquired in early childhood, it seems to be specially indicative of this stage of development, as will be established later. In puberty, significantly changed relations can very often be observed. The case that concerns us here can now be easily explained by Raimund's attitude to his father. This conditions a linkage between the realistic description and the fantasy contents (father's promise). With his father's help, R. had learned to adapt his wishes to reality and could not avoid this censorship in his fantasies as well. Deviation from reality, i.e., any modification of the facts is made unnecessary by the firm belief in the father's promise.

Raimund's infantile material is very rich. His father is a lover of horses and an experienced driver. Strong impressions from R.'s childhood speak for the choice of his father as ego-ideal, and in the game under consideration this ideal became real. R. identified himself with his father—at least at first—in realistic thinking.

Even before R. recognized the above facts in analysis, he again asked himself, 'But why was there a change at all?' and soon after "yes, why did my father not buy me the goat?" In the course of dealing with this second question, R.'s further part in the game became clear.

R. had not been given the goat. After a time the interest he had shewn at the first encounter diminished because, in spite of all his efforts, he could no longer get to see the goat ε.. l cart. (Our inquiries revealed that it had soon been resold to another owner). Thus phase 2 of the game became one of revenge on the father. It took the form of Raimund's leaving the parents' house, migrating to the grandmother, and lowering his social class (R. becomes carrier, builder, day-laborer, "cheese-monger"), while making himself materially independent.

The denial of R.'s wish evidently meant to him the withdrawal of his father's love, and he responded in kind. But estrangement from the father afforded him considerable self-reliance (flow of the freed libido back into the ego), so that he released himself from the frustrating environment and its objects. The migration only as far as the grandmother's house betrays some reservation about this decision. (Some family history, that cannot be gone into here, naturally also played a part in this choice.)

Insight into all the details of the transition from phase 1 to phase 2 unfortunately remains denied to us. We think, however, that knowledge of the motive for the change in play content means a large step forward, since it is now feasible to penetrate the second phase. To be sure, one significant part of phase 1 is still unexplained: how did it come about that one individual's experience was accepted by other players as *their* theme as well? Did this group acceptance effect any change in it?

The widespread explanations of children's play groups, which demand sometimes inadmissible and sometimes useless hypotheses about play drives, social instincts, etc., fail to explain groups which exhibit such ephemeral phenomena as *fantasy play*. As was pointed out above, R.'s memories of play, substantiated and deepened by analysis, could explain almost all the contents of the game, so that this content itself was seen to constitute a mirror image of R.'s own experience. The participation of two other children, unrelated to R., however, requires further explanation. One almost assumes that at just about the time of their acceptance an actual frustration (similar to that experienced by R) evoked in the co-players similar reactions, so that partial identity of content and determinants was followed by identity of results. This simple possibility, perhaps credible for two siblings, cannot be considered here. Apart from the quite different familial and social structure of the circle from which Josef and his sister came, no such statement was made by the participants, nor did observation suggest anything similar. Josef's taking part in Raimund's fantasies about his wishes for the he-goat and their expression in play, can therefore certainly not be seen as the result of the very same situation that we came to recognize above as decisive for R. Rather, we are obliged to look for other determinants of J.'s interest in the game.

J.'s parents are day-laborers, living in a gloomy kitchen and sitting room; R.'s parents are well-to-do shop keepers. In answer to a casual question (at the time I was recording R.'s memories) as to what had so favored the friendship between R. and J., R.'s mother replied approximately: "J.'s parents shopped with us; they often owed money and paid in installments. A good understanding between the children was seen to be desirable by J.'s parents." After I had listened to J., and did not conceal my surprise at this response from R.'s mother, she said: "Yes, he is now in X (a big town) and only on leave here; he still owes us money and therefore wants to be helpful." We must not take this information too seriously, as R.'s mother was often worried about the ability of her debtors to pay. But it is not impossible that we can read from it an actual presented motive for the growing intimacy J. and his sister experienced with R. Some remarks of R.'s and a few general observations cause us to believe that precisely this egoistic motive, perhaps stimulated in part by his parents, was animating J. Friendships of proletarian with bourgeois children are very often directed less to persons than to the material resources they symbolize. Proletarian children are often welcome to the bourgeois as tractable objects on whom fantasies of domination and power can be brought to bear. This relation, naturally only one of many possible to describe, corresponds to that shared by R. and J.

The individual elements in the play content turned out to be unimportant to J., not derived from his moods. Thus his motive for joining in R.'s fantasies must be sought elsewhere. The game is thus to be seen only as a means used by J. to attain a definite end: it represents the wish to be rich, i.e., to live like a wealthy child, more precisely, like R. Understood in this way, J.'s behavior then becomes clear to us. R.'s story and "game" are a welcome opportunity for J. to make these wishes conscious and to gratify them by hallucination.

In phase 1, this fantasied gratification is relatively difficult, the distance from reality being too great, and J.'s identification with R. is not very successful. It can be helped, however, by interchange of roles. Thus, at one time, R. is coachman and J. 'Sir' and, at another time, these roles are reversed. J. is more silent and lacks initiative. He shares the fantasies but cannot speak, perhaps because these fantasies do not hold their ground with his censor (reality-testing) and are therefore shut off from the motor system of speech. Perhaps because such undisguised contents are not often suitable for verbal repetition in fantasy play, this tends to be an ephemeral phenomenon and perhaps this "game" might also have come to an end after a short time if the conditions in which the play group existed had not been significantly favored by R.'s reaction to his father's refusal. Only now was a closer approach made possible for

J., an approach that did not make excessive demands on his ability to fantasize because R. now played the poverty-stricken and forsaken one, the one who was himself drawn toward J. and his family. Herewith a basis for easier identification is created for J. The tendency of R. to flee from his parents' home, deeply grounded in his early childhood, now finds a favorable medium in the group. (Raimund's statements had already made me aware of the importance to him of the change of parents. Analysis had now releaved this as a typical reaction of R. to his father. For instance, at 4 years of age, after a painful scene, he did in fact run away spontaneously to his grandmother's house.) Perhaps this favorable constellation of wishes tended to "a discharge of psychic tension through play" and thus saved the psychic apparatus from further complex expenditure. The biological value of play is again proved by these considerations which, at the same time, explain the partial or total abandonment of play by sick children.

PSYCHOLOGICAL MEANING OF FANTASIES IN LATENCY

The material available to us, scanty in yield but surprisingly consistent, compels us to accept that the stage of development that Freud called the latency period (6-13 years of age) offers extremely favorable conditions for the production of fantasy play. Naturally we can observe fantasies much earlier, but these are nearly always accompanied by actions and are seldom called games.

According to Freud, latency is to be conceived as a period of the covering-over of infantile sexual impulses, accounted for by inability to procreate during this biological phase. Repression has proved itself to be the most important mechanism in bringing about this superstructure; at least the other possible vicissitudes of instinct, such as sublimation, cannot be demonstrated to anything like the same degree. Disgust and shame have shown themselves to be the most important reaction-formations that protect the child exhibitionist, voyeur, and coprophiliac from his drives and make him socially tolerable. The possibility of satisfying the drive at another level is offered by retreat from reality and flight (or fixation) to fantasy.

This drive-satisfaction can free the individual of all hindrances and leaves it to the choice of the fantasy weaver (and to the strength of his reality-testing) whether to fantasize about the obstacles in his way, or about overcoming or circumventing them. In some cicumstances active reality-testing can be retained even within the fantasy.

Undoubtedly, this process gives rise to stages in returning to reality from fantasy life ranging from autism to socialization (cf. Anna Freud 1922). But there is also the possibility of easing or adjusting unsuccessful or early infantile repression by means of fantasy, while the actual repressions of this period of life are duly carried on (through disgust and shame). In all the fantasy games we have investigted, childish megalomania, omnipotence of thought, and similar features of the narcissistic-animistic stage indicate typical unsuccessful repression in earliest infancy. It is known that the enduringly pleasurable formation of the first childish love relationship, carries in it a renunciation of certain personal inclinations, since object-libido demands a sacrifice of ego-libido. This sacrifice consists in the child's giving up a set of his own wishes, and being compensated for this renunciation by the affection and thanks of the beloved person. A voluntary impoverishment of the ego thus takes place as a means of attaining an object. In fantasy games a number of such renunciations now appear reversed. Indeed they are characterized by the tendency of the players not to display impoverishment or renunciation but to impress one another and do great deeds. Naturally, other games display the same tendency, but, as will be shown, the process seems to reach its peack in fantasy play.

Greta Wiesenthal's description of her fantasy play (1919) illuminates this point.

> But another room seemed to me even more remarkable because it had a wardrobe built into the wall and this was the starting-point of all my dreams about underground castles.
>
> Hitherto I had only known doors that led to other rooms. But a door which opened and had no room behind it, only a semi-dark mysterious niche, that was something I had never seen before. In my fantasy I took possession of this wall cupboard and it became for me the entrance to an underground castle, to which a secret

door led down which only I knew about. There, in this wonderful castle, I had the most beautiful games that my wish to play could think out. It also occurred to me to tell my sisters that I was not really the child of my parents but had been brought by a fairy and my true home was the underground castle. My sister listened to these tales with close attention, agreed to everything, and knew no more what was true and what was false than I did myself. Only the sister nearest to me in age, with whom, I belive, I was on very close terms, said rightly that it was a bit too much that I should not be her true sister, and I took care afterwards not to lay too much weight on this part of the story. It was certainly much more important that we should not disturb our ability to make up stories.

At my request for further information, Mrs. Martha Wiesenthal stated that a similar game later contained the following variation: "Each sister crept under a bed and told tales there about the castle she owned, whereby great competition arose between the sisters, each trying to outdo the others in fantasies." Although the success of these fantasies was ego-inflating, their being misunderstood or pooh-poohed by the fellow-players meant a mortification—just as any criticism from the environment, which impaired the power of the fantasy makers, itself constituted a personal hurt. But this could be a means of actualizing feelings of guilt which on their side again exercised censorship on the game and could allow it to fade away.

Here Grete Wiesenthal's autobiography (1919) provides another valuable example.

"One day, when I was sitting up with my sister on a stool, which was supposed to stand in front of a piano, completely absorbed in playing the piano four-handed, the door opened and a friend of my mother's entered and came up to me, indignant and angry. In her hair a twig of lilac nodded, accompanying the frantic movements of her head, at which I had to gaze in fascination the whole time she was talking to me. She said, "Now Gretel, these are really fine things that one has to hear about you. What lies do you tell my cook? That you will only marry a prince? You school girl, you goose, to tell her you had diamonds and pearls? You liar. That you would only drive in a carriage? You vain monkey, this can't go on. Whatever will become of you?" These accusations turned to further thunder at my parents.

This time, too, I did not feel any guilt and the remarkable thing was that during this admonitory sermon I felt deeply ashamed of the nakedness of my feet. And yet up till then I had been so pleased to go barefoot, like so many of my school fellows. From this day on I knew that it is dangerous to entrust one's dreams to other people."

How much less often fantasies designated as "games" come under censorship from adults and children, than those which apparently correspond to reality (pseudologia), will be described later. At present, however, the analysis of content is still in the foreground of our deliberations.

If we refer to the preponderance of wishes of a narcissistic nature, we are naturally only emphasizing a characteristic of all games belonging to this period of development, though certainly more than that has been done before. Fantasy games are just the kind of play in which the narcissistic fixation of the individual seeks to remain free of conflict and for the most part can remain so. This can be made plain by considering the economics of fantasy: "It is during this period of total or only partial latency that are built up the mental forces which are later to impede the course of sexual instinct and, like dams, restrict its flow—disgust, feelings of shame and the claims of aesthetic and moral ideals" (Freud, 1905). Because of this repressive thrust the demands on the ego, the initiator of repression (Freud, 1914) are exceptionally heavy. Throughout the latency period, internal forces are at work to lighten the repressive labor of the ego. Thus earlier repressions, initiated to overcome the animistic-narcissistic stage, are loosened or even cancelled. The first result of renunciation of the oedipal object is enhancement of the ego, if the process runs its course without noticeable disturbance. Hence the general weight of repression is not only reduced by the diminution of earlier repressions but also constitutes a counterpressure in the service of the new set of repressions.

It seems that it is just in fantasy play, with its obvious wishfulfillments so useful to the ego, that the last reserves, so to speak, are engaged at the end of latency. In any case, the undistorted wishes, just because they are undisguised, do least harm to the psychic equilibrium. They after all only strengthen the barrier which the latency period raises aginst its actual partner, the sexual instinct.

If the meaning of the fantasies and the point in time of their appearance have been successfully outlined, we must now consider what influences are required to drive the fantasies into the particular form of fantasy play.

FANTASY AND ITS RELATION TO REALITY AND REPRESSION

As expected, the people who made statements could give no reason for having labeled their cooperation in fantasying as "play." At least they answered in recalling that they continued to meet at agreed times "just because it was so enjoyable." Hence we conclude tha knowledge of the motivations for playing a fantasy game is to be sought elsewhere than in the statements of the players. Consider first of all to the site of the game. All the statements confirm that the play site was carefully and intentionally kept apart from adults and strange children and chosen for its privacy. One of the speakers mentioned explicitly, "Julie told me this and suddenly somebody knocked on the door. (The door was always locked at the beginning of the game.) Before opening it we quickly took up the doll, to conceal that we were playing a fantasy game." The "he-goat" game was played in a dark room; Frau Martha Wiesenthal relates that each player crept under a bed, and so on.

We can assume two different reasons for the fantasy players' timidity regarding the world around them: (1) In connection with a group of games hitherto known as "secret games," the content of the fantasies had to be forbidden, or at least some part of it had to contain forbidden elements; (2) the illusory reality is in danger of being destroyed by adults. Our data offer little support for the first assumption. I have observed only one instance of a forbidden presentation given by a play group: "Two sisters are travelling on a ship. The shipfounders and the sisters swim to an island. They get a child and look for coconuts—then some black men arrive who will not let them go." Later, when another friend joined the sisters in their game, "Three old spinsters get—no, find—a child. It is called Karl and now they bring it up. When he is about two years old, he is still forever wetting his pants. This is very naughty and we force him to use the pot." It must be said that, in comparison with other games, such undisguised presentations take a back seat in fantasy play.

From here then we are led to our assumption 2, which will clarify the secret nature of fantasy play still further. If fantasies are a substitute satisfaction for frustration, they must not, after all, be brought into relation to whatever caused or evoked the frustration. In addition to the ego, such instigators include the parents, educators, and the social environment of the child (Freud, 1914). All repressions are codetermined by these instigators, all misstatements tested by them. In fantasy play the ego makes use of erlier rejected ego impulses, without always being able to take the amount of care necessary completely to misrepresent them, care which it must exert just now for the overcoming of infantile sexual impulses. It is less concerned to conceal the ego impulses, against which it must wage the final battle, than to conceal the immediate enemy, namely the sexual impulses, against which it leads these others into battle.

A strong ego is required to overcome the sexual repression in the latency period. We can conceive that, in order to achieve this, the narcissistic positions that were abandoned at the beginning of the latency period become ever more important during its course and take possession very forcefully toward its end. In this way, as we have already indicated, infantile repressions (narcissism) become lightened for the benefit of the current task of repression. We see this alleviation very clearly in fantasy play. Its being hidden from the outer world (except for fellow players) allows it to be maintained, since by this time, if anything serious occurs, like facing adults, reality-testing is sufficiently acute to perceive its fantastic nature. But this insight would worsen the position of the ego in regard to its task of repression. Hiding the fantasies, however, does not seem to be the only means the child seizes on to maintain them before himself and the outer world. The fantasies, so they can continue to exist at least in the group, are given a disarming name, i.e., "play." Elsewhere it could be argued that the criteria for the distinction of play from work are in no way exclusively psychological; doubtless other important reasons must have arisen in the primeval era of mankind which led to the separation of play from work in concept and in speech. Just as there are occasions on which children excuse the act of onanism by saying "I was only playing," so the declaration "play" guarantees the possibility of removing, within the group, the inhibitions which prevent the discharge of the orgiastic megalomania of the child. Thus the child uses every means of maintaining the important privilege of childhood to fantasize, but here too, as we see, he makes concessions to the world of adults in giving his serious fantasy world the stamp of adult valuation: it is "play." It cannot be denied that in some other expressions of children of this age, like playing at theater, the same formative conditions also rule. Certainly these are to be sought in the roles of the actors and the intensity with which the roles are played. Fantasy play makes use of a completely undisguised presentation of the players as principals and dispenses with names, dressing-up, and similar technicalities. Thereby it loses in reality value and can exist only in a circle of a few confidants.

That fantasies will be construed as lies can be gathered from Grete Wiesenthal's communications. Discussion of the dynamic relationship between daydream, creation, and pseudologia fantastica (this alone can be considered here) was successfully opened by Dr. Helene Deusch (1922): "The day dream is kept secret because its contradiction of reality is constantly known to the dreamer." In poetic creation, on the contrary, the form is found in which "the barriers between his ego and that of others is bridged. Thus [the poet's] psychic tensions are freed and he also stirs them in us and in this way enables us to share in the enjoyment of his poetic day dreams." This condition of aesthetic enjoyment is missing in pseudologia (habitual, apparently motiveless, lying), as in the ordinary waking dream. The fact that pseudologia levels the contradiction between its content and the real situation makes contact with reality possible, in that it makes reality values more acceptable. Helene Deutsch adds, "The waking dreamer is indeed also inclined to hold that his phantasy is true, and this is also the condition of enjoyment, though the feeling of reality seems to be much more dominant, intense and alluring in pseudologia, and so it possesses the power to represent phantasy productios to others as truth." In this sense, fantasy play can be thought of as pseudologia which only retains its reality value for a small circle of the like-minded. The power of the inner over the outer world, which is so characteristic of pseudologists, has not attained such strength in fantasy play. This is probably because some amount of object libidinal satisfaction must be obtained from it. What is certain about it is that the fantasies can still be inhibited by the outer world, by objects.

FANTASY PLAY VS.
DAYDREAM AND ARTISTIC CREATION

The foregoing remarks about an ephemeral but nevertheless typical and characteristic phenomenon of the later period of latency, have pointed to some dynamic relationship with the poetic creativity of children and young people.

Freud designated as an important fundamental difference between fiction and daydream the latter's being kept secret. A poem, if also hidden, is allways conceived of as coming to be known by other people, even if only by one person, the friend, the beloved. Fantasy play takes a middle position between these two extremes. It occurs indeed in a group, and is the secret of its several members, but at the same time a considerable effort is made to keep the content of the game secret. We are inclined to look upon this effort as the successful reaction formation to powerful wishes for esteem and fredom of action. Though such egoistic and narcissistic tendencies are involved in our games as render valuable service to the ego, they can appear before the outer world and its censorship only in disguise—as games and creative writing (the latter by individual children). Wishes appear almost undistorted, they are almost always told in the first person, and restraints in presentations and censorship of egoistic wishes are still forgone. Closer enquiry reveals (we base ourselves here on Raimund's goat game) that the same fantasies that appear in the game were earlier experienced as daydreams. The individual daydream becomes the daydream of the group. What Bernfeld denoted as the most pschologically important of the poetic processes—tertiary elaboration—is lacking here. The standards and preconditions which function for the reproductions of adolescent and adult poets for recall in disguised and concealed form are not yet present. Mention must not be omitted of the fact that not one of our informants could refer to any such production of poems. On the other hand a relationship between the content of fantasy play and children's poetry is not to be overlooked. Both are concerned mainly with the satisfaction of ambitious and self-seeking instinctual impulses. The question as to what conditions favor or hinder the choice of one or the other must be added to the many further problems for research.

11

The Archaic in Play

PRIMITIVE INITIATION RITES AND
BOYS "PLAYING AT SOLDIERS"

Education and training in our time are based on the relationship of individual pupils to individual teachers. Children's natural group-formations acquire practical educational importance occasionally but only insofar as they can be made to serve the education of each individual child. A child is left within a group in the hope that this will favor the educational result that was not attainable in the "ideal" individual upbringing. Alternatively, the children are grouped in order to treat them, owing to the shortage of teachers, as a single object, and, once the goal is attained, to divide them into as many single individuals as there were before. Because, in practical education, the group is not an end in itself but a means to an end, up to now psychological investigations of such social manifestations have not been able to offer more than a description of their effect on the single individual.

An inborn social instinct and imitation are posited as motives for natural sociability and, for prepubertal children, a further pragmatic motive is the prospect of successful competition. The assertions about motives are not only onesided and inadequate because the observer has approached insufficient material from one point of view. They are also inadequate because of the difficulties of registering such data, owing to the way in which such children's societies form and break up again, and because of the belief engendered in us by tradition and social custom that children belong to the family. It would be quite wrong to transfer conceptions of association from the life of adults to childhood, though in truth we may hope to be able to say more about society formations in childhood and youth when we know more about those of adults.

An example of the possible significance of such childhood groups can be seen in the following example of a group of boys' play, as illuminated by the deeper understanding of the true motives of associations in childhood to be found in Freud's *Totem and Taboo* (1913), Reik's "The Puberty Rites of Savages (on some correspondences between the psychic life of savages and neurotics)" (1928) and Erwin Kohn's "The Initiation Rites of the Historical Professions" (1922).

Our soldier games, my three young informants told me in 1921, were played within a short distance of the town (a small country town) on the hills, small woods, and rocks, where we used earlier to hold our bat and ball games, then "cops and robbers" and whatever else boys play. Once (in the war year 1916) there was a group of twelve- to fourteen-year-olds, who played soldiers intensively and were much envied by us, since we were still in part pupils at the elementary school. It was no ordinary war game, in which two parties form up who hunt and fall upon one another, fight and are defeated or triumph, English and Boers—before the war—or Austrians and Serbs in the world war; we also had such games. This group had military caps, medals, one of them a scabbard, a corded cover, all kinds of discarded or useless articles of military equipment. They drilled to commands which they had heard about from soldiers on leave or relatives, lined up in open order and had a medical orderly and two girls with Red Cross armbands, a transport service corps, sometimes also a dog, who was meant to carry messages and "munitions." They almost always played only against an assumed enemy, stormed the rocks, dug trenches at the edge of the wood, all under the command of a certain boy (a fourteen-year-old). We were only allowed to look on from a distance, if we did not want to be thrashed, but we wished very much that we could be permitted to take part.

Our wish was soon fulfilled. We became recruits and were trained, shouted at, and had to do press-ups and stretch up and down; we tolerated this but sometimes left the "exercise ground" in tears. After a few days we were told we must join in a maneuver and would then be sworn in. To this the colors were taken along, which had hitherto been hidden by one of the co-players.

The maneuver: we were drawn up in rank and file and had to march and run, so that some could hardly keep up; there was much grumbling. Because we could do too little, the maneuver was called off and postponsed to one of the next days. Many of the older boys declared the little ones were useless and we should again be excluded. Then the game began afresh and this time we all tried very hard.

Then it was announced that the field service exercise would now take place. Four guard posts were set up in a rectangle near a road, and two guard posts with the Red Cross nurses were installed in the wood where the hospital was. We were given the job of crawling along the roadside ditch, keeping ourselves well hidden and then crawling across the road, where some of the bigger boys stood and hit us on the back if we did not bend low enough. On the other side of the road the ditch continued on to a water conduit. Here there was a cement pipe, through which we little ones could just manage to crawl. But it was stuffed with straw and hay and newspaper, and one of the boys had put in some horse dung; it was wet inside too so they had probably pissed into it. We had to collect, crouched down, outside the entrance and at this moment one of us received a blow because he was not bent low enough and was kicked out. Then all the big boys came together and stationed themselves in rank and file at the other end of the conduit. We were very excited at being ordered to crawl through a perhaps two-and-a-half-meter-long conduit, stopped up in this way. We only did it in order to become permanent co-players. When we came out the other end the big boys gave a salute of honor, the flag was raised high, and one boy put his hand to his mouth like a trumpet. Thus, in something like a general march, we were quickly arranged in rank and file and had to "swear at sea, on land, and in the air"; we were then dismissed from our lines, the Red Cross nurses were again present, and there was a rest.

Any attempt to find rational motives for this soldier game would have to begin with the phenomenon described as a "maneuver" where I think it may well founder. This obviously significant and real part of the game, inexplicable by simple imitation, this "mixture of jest and cruelty, of sense and nonsense, of solemnity and the grotesque" such as Erwin Kohn adduces for the initiation rites of the historical craftsman's guilds, makes it reasonable to assume here and to investigate an inner relationship between these historical boys' ceremonies (consecration of apprentices, dubbing of knights, admission of students) and those of primitive people. According to Rank and Roheim (1932), who observed primitive initiation rites in the field, the event took place as follows: the youngster who has attained manhood is taken away from his mother and in the longhouse, near the tribal settlement, undergoes a varying period of instruction in war and hunting customs, the laws and rituals of the tribe, in order finally, in a ceremonial and terrifying rite of circumcision, to be declared "marriageable" and enrolled in the male society. Roheim found the most important stages in the basic training customs among the Australian tribes he investigated to be separation of the boys from their mothers, instruction in the customs of the tribe, ceremonial circumcision, the festival of rebirth. The boy receives a new name, he does not recognize his mother any more, and the whole event is played out in total separation from women. The mothers mourn their sons as dead.

While the primitive and historical initiations of all kinds are rites firmly established by tribal custom, we can see, if we will, in the ceremonies of our children's play, that they enter as spontaneous, single and temporary events, not overlaid by deliberate obscuring rationalization for cultural purposes, as in many customs such as confirmation, entrance examinations, etc.

First let us ask whether and how far we are concerned here with a boys' initiation ceremony. A closed and exclusive group of older boys is faced by a group of younger ones, full of envy and longing. The younger boys show their desire to share in the doings of the older ones possibly by some banal imitation, similar to what I described between seniors and juniors in a gymnastic group (Chap. 5).

Perhaps, one or two years later, they might even succeed in forming a worthwhile, rival group of their own. The tribal elders' possession of priority rights to war and hunt booty and women would have been continually threatened by the rising generation of boys if they had not obviated this threat of death by accepting the boys when they grew to manhood and sharing women and possessions with them. The weakening of their power and influence by death, illness or by the wounding of strong men in battle or the chase, was made good by the intake of younger men. Our play group was also strengthened by this addition, eliminating envious competitors at the same time. Finally, it also acquired a number of boys prepared to suffer, ready and willing to expose their lives to the cruel impulses of the war-minded. The prospect of enrollment in this group of soldier players induced endurance of the conditions of acceptance, so that the active co-worker could emerge from the passive spectator.

But the apprenticeship is not merely instruction in exercising and soldierly behavior. Anyone who sees it through furnishes evidence of his efficiency and therewith also brings before the eyes of the older the dangerousness of the younger one. He must, on one occasion, be truly made aware of the strength and power of the group of elders, as if only then could the real honor and the real appreciation of belonging to it be established. Then it is asserted, "We have no fear of you whippersnappers, but if you recognize our supremacy and pass the test we have set for you, then you can join us and wear the military caps, whistles, and rifle cases we have hitherto mercilessly kept from you."

But the meaning of these acceptance ceremonies is not yet exhausted. As with those of savages and medieval craftsmen, they fall into two parts, one that serves as preparation and one that is the enrollment itself. What strikes us above all is the behavior toward women. Among savages the young men are isolated. If they may meet women at all it is only those with veiled faces; if they see a woman's footmark, they must jump over it. The women, in particular the mothers of these boys, must turn their faces away or hide themselves if they are approaching. According to the apparently milder usages of the Middle Ages, women might at most be present as spectators; in our game they were given secure cover in the wood. The cover seemed to serve less as protection from enemy attack than as defense against the curiosity of the Red Cross nurses.

What role did the girls play, and why should the boys defend themselves against their curiosity? Before we try to find an answer I should like to refer to another piece of evidence that women are definitely excluded from boys' initiation ceremonies or substitute rites.

THE DREAM OF OPERATION
AS INITIATION RITE

In the course of treatment of a young man, whose transition from puberty to adulthood was not proceeding successfully on its own, it emerged that he was suffering from a constriction of the foreskin (phimosis) which made the operative treatment necessary. The night after the operation, about which his concern and anxiety had been proved to be largely excessive, he has this dream: "I am in the operating theater and am being washed before the operation. Then men come up to me, throw me onto the operating table and, holding my hands and feet, begin to plane me. [A student custom which consisted in the person to be executed being "planed" on a table.] Nearby the professor was sharpening a huge knife and at the moment he approaches me the nurse leaves the room and I wake, dripping with sweat from anxiety."

The dream, into whose individual analysis I do not wish to enter here, again contains some of those elements recognized by us in pubertal rites which, like the analytic literature, were not known to the dreamer: these elements include above all the preparation for the operation, a mixture of day remainders and cruel deeds, beginning with the planing, a kind of reminiscence of childhood punishments, and finally the threatening with the knife—all of which make the patient unable to dream to the end so that he withdraws from it in anxiety by waking. Finally, there is the departure of the nurse precisely at the time the professor approaches menacingly with the knife. If the initiation rites also contain a castration ceremony and the anxiety of the patient is about that and not about the operation, we can bring our game into relation to it without difficulty and see in it the final renunciation of the incestuously desired mother, the cutting off—the equivalent of cutting round (circumcision)—being the indicated allusion to castration. This has the meaning, which remains unconscious, of punishment of the forbidden and repressed longings for one's own mother and sister and is the conscious sign of being made free for sexual intercourse with women other than blood relations. The employment of both tendencies gives it a structure like that of a neurotic symptom, a similarity which has repeatedly been demonstrated in religious ceremonies. In addition, the women's keeping at a distance can be seen as their agreement with the "circumcisers" and the renunciation of motherly care.

Let us return now to the question why the girls were excluded from the ritual act itself, the ceremony of acceptance. I inquired about this from my informants, but the only answer I got was the one which, being a rationalization, was close at hand; in service in the field, the medics are in the rear. Among savages there are strong prohibitions to prevent meetings between women and the marriageable youngster. These are interpreted as measures directed against the incestuous wishes of mothers and sons. But it seems to me that there is also a pointer therein to the sexual attitude of women in the tribe. I think it is a measure against women's curiosity. If circumcision represents symbolic castration, and the dominance of the man over the women rests on the high estimation of the genitals, then the women would have every reason to consider themselves castrated men. But we assume that the deed the ritual represents was once real and therefore that the primeval fathers sometimes castrated or killed their sons. The mystery of becoming a female would thus be unveiled for women in this process of castration. The women's curiosity directed itself to this ceremony, its analogue in our game being the curiosity of the two girls. That it was their extreme curiosity about the behavior of the boys which brought the girls into their games may well be assumed. The meaning of the symbolic unmanning would be lost if the boys were reminded too much of the symbolic, not actual, event: the presence of girls, if unconsciously regarded as actually mutilated persons, might affect the play or make-believe atmosphere of the acceptance ritual, making it more threatening and rousing too vivid castration anxieties. The boys' male-leaguing, homosexual tendencies, which could be yet another reason for the girls' curiosity, could not be given satisfaction, and finally the novices would expose themselves to the ridicule of the girls or to a renewal of their motherly solicitude. After all, the last and most important aim of the initiation rites is to transform the boy dependent on the mother into the man superior to her.

All that remains to be explained is the last act of the "maneuver." We know that among primitive peoples, some tribes make use of most artistically constructed monsters into whose mouth the boys must disappear to re-emerge through the tail end in a symbolic re-birth. At the apprentice tests, the candidate had to crawl under a stool; in our game through a pipe stuffed with hay, straw, and ordure. Is this not the identical representation of rebirth, and is not the one under test received with full honours at the other end of the pipe, like a new and different person? I think that those unschooled in psychoanalysis should nevertheless follow our work in those regions adjacent to psychoanalytic therapy in which the immediate effect of interpretation and the final healing result of the total work on the illness cannot be pursued but where psychoanalytic research has begun to shed a bright light on the hitherto unknown.

THE MEANING OF THE ARCHAIC
IN CHILDREN'S PLAY

The question of the genesis of our boys' play is neither an ethnological nor an historical one. Sociology and history offer us only material for comparison but no explanation for its coming into being, because it is not a matter of a traditional game. On the contrary one could assume that, in our cultural circles too, some individuals still retain in their unconscious the ability to experience and describe specific events, often of an insignificant nature, in a form patterned in primeval times. Such manifestations are known in the pathological anatomy of man, i.e., in the organic aspect of the body. For instance, parts of persisting embryonic gills sometimes occur in the region of the human neck. In circumstances still not fully known, these can give rise to a malignant growth (carcinoma, cancer). Why should such partial, persistent archaic residues not also be found in the domain of the psychic, and in what form can they make their appearance?

The child's play is very often the form in which the archaic manifests itself. Psychoanalysis, which took its point of departure from the effects of experience, that is to say the contact of young people with the outer world, very soon decided to consider also these indwelling, archaic reaction-formations in human beings. Their content is the primeval fantasies of mankind, and the form some of them take is the archaic thinking of the magico-animistic stage. This thinking in neurotics can be activated by experience and can form symptoms; in psychotics, it can lead to a kind of self-healing when their relation to reality has been disturbed. In the child, it appears quite regularly in play. To some extent it always accompanies our rational, logical thinking itself; in part the archaic has grown into the logical. An attempt to understand the content of a game solely in the light of personal experience would mean renouncing all these manifestations.

Stanley Hall (1924), starting from the theory of transmission by descent, formulated a theory of play in which he held the view that only atavistic, rudimentary functions were generally used in play. They atrophy before final maturation but live out their life beforehand in play, just as the tail of a tadpole must grow before it withers and thereby stimulates the growth of the legs, which would otherwise not grow. In general the types of children's games and stories succeed one another, like the new main preoccupations in the cultural history of mankind. Another American psychologist, Carr (1902) introduced the hypothesis of catharsis into his theory of play, thinking that it is mainly the asocial, instinctual demands, useless for practical purposes, that find expression and discharge in play. The idea that the residues of human prehistory are superfluous at present and merely represent memorials is erroneous, and it is incorrect to compare them to malformations of the body, such as the web between two fingers of a neonate. Archaic traits can be demonstrated throughout the physical, as in the psychic, depending only on the refinement of the methods employed.

The language of play and the ciphers by means of which it is transmitted—the action contained in it—is always copied from generation to generation, like renewing the writing on a gravestone, and the original meaning is often lost in this way. For instance, the doll is a plaything known to all people throughout the ages. It is missing only when the little girls have to undertake the care of children at a very early age. This, in turn, depended not only on whether the mother had to go out to other work but also on the unconscious valuation placed on the child, for example, whether the child was regarded a common possession of the tribe or as a wicked demon, whether it must be protected from the father by the mother. The magical theories that clung about the childqere transferred to much more harmless things, to wood or to cloth, and in them the archaic notions set firm so that they survive until today in toys. Some games could enable one to trace the path that leads from prehistory to children's play. What is depicted in play was once real patricide, incest, rape, and the killing of children. From the real deed one went over to religious or folk festivals and cultural customs. These then became the play of adults; they were described by poets in myths, sagas, and fairy tales and finally taken over by children in play.

In his well-known psychoanalytic inquiry into children's play, Pfeifer (1919) establishes a connection between the game "Fox into the hole" and an Australian magical fertility rite and compares it with the unconscious meaning of mythological and historical customs. He can show, for example, that, when the Free States were founded, prevention and punishment were given to the criminal first of all for sexual offenses, for incest. The old prescriptions for religious ceremonial, the entrenched tribal customs, can be found again in the obsessional rituals of the sick. Pfeifer also draws attention to this, underlining the "obsessional character" of the rules of play. In all our circular, skipping, and peg games we should surmise remnants of old cultural customs; their psychic effects find expression in children as in the ecstatic dances of savages.

Toys for very young children, which immemorial tradition has sought to preserve for them, must not be forgotten here. Are these different types of rattle designed only to serve the exercise of the senses? Is not ancient history otherwise full of mystical theories and magical gestures relating to early childhood? So can we not also see in the clappers and bells, whistles and trumpets of remnants of old animistic-magical times, when noise-making instruments were feared magical instruments? Does not the little child's feelings of omnipotence also obtain visible expression through them, and are these children not also medicine men and wizards? The behavior of adult obsessionals, the magical formulae and gestures with which a certain inner calming is connected, and even more, the fantasy-creations of psychotics and the products of their hallucinations, can support such a conception. It is admittedly scarcely possible to bring forward more than occasional proof in justification of this supposition. If we wish to prove the importance of the experiences of early childhood to the pedagogue, we urge him to be analyzed himself, to observe children and to analyze adults. The archaic is indeed buried under too many layers, and so mixed up with later experience, for it to be systematically presented. Nevertheless its significance cannot be ignored because without a knowledge of the archaic the games would not be completely understandable, and furthermore in the archaic is embedded the history of the Oedipus complex, on whose mastery the child's health or illness, educational success or failure, are known to depend.

12

Child and Fairy Tales

The point of view that psychoanalysis offers nothing but a description of sexuality is so widespread among educators that it is necessary to assert that this is a misrepresentation of Freud's intention and achievement. Surely one should not limit the significance of psychoanalytic thinking about the unconscious so easily.

Speaking about fairy tales demands inquiry into their relationship to unconscious material, which returns disguised to consciousness or comes to light in poetry as in neurotic symptoms or the dreams of normal persons. For what excites the thinking of the human being and stimulates action or composition, are not only perceptions from outside but also those constantly arising from within, the impulses of his instincts. It is these which drive him to the outer world, which he readily perceives and with which he must come to terms. He takes a part of it into himself and his instinct shapes itself to it, as a river to its course through the countryside.

When the older investigators of fairy tales wanted to see in them the elaboration of primitive man's attitude to nature, they still had in mind only the natural events in the outer world and not those in the inner world. This they could not see because they lacked the instrument of psychoanalysis and also, perhaps, the courage to take into account these internal natural happenings. But it is expected that pedagogues keep these happenings, the instinctual life of the child, forever pressing for expression, invisible and covered up. When psychoanalysis, like the natural sciences, shows educators the kind of "material" with which they must work, it furnishes them also with arguments for refusing the superhuman task being required of them; it helps too to lessen the merciless overpowering of the child by strong adults. Through helping to shatter the notion that the child is completely good or innocent, it does away with the opposition between child and adult. It prevents the disillusionment and the cruel reactions to which incorrect, idealized concepts must lead.

If we assess the fairy tale from this point of view, we must admit with astonishment how much it shows us about children, and, while it appears to us all too primitively constructed, we can at the same time harness it to our educational machinery. We must first put aside the adverse valuation of the fairy tale as a means of education and refrain from requiring that the noncontemporary, unrealistic, fantastic aspects of the tale be eliminated or modified. As psychoanalysts, we will not interest ourselves, as do the psychologists, in the construction and further development of the child's imagination (the way in which he perceives his environment) but in how his unconscious reacts, and in how he controls his instinctual life, since it is on this control that his future well-being and social functioning depend.

Our first question concerns the conditions of origin of fairy tales—folk-stories, sagas, and myths. We think here of their sources in the unconscious and refuse to trace these back to a single determining factor for such a complex, literary structure, as the old fairy tale research has mostly done. In their psychoanalytic investigations Riklin (1908), Abraham (1909), Rank (1919) and Federn (1924) called the fairy tale a gateway to the unconscious of mankind, just as Freud found the dream the most fruitful path to the unconscious of the individual.

Like Freud in his study of the dream, these authors took as their starting point the conception that fairy tales are thoroughly meaningful, in that in them wishes, conceptions, anticipations and anxieties—instinctual demands in general—find expression. The fairy tales that are best known and most used in education are works of art. With definite social and pedagogic intent, they wear a dress that should satisfy our demands for comprehensibility and persuasive power. Just as we can trace the manifest content of a dream back through various layers to its latent content, and hence to the sources of the dream, fairy-tale research has been able to prove that each of our tales has a series of precursors, older versions. However, their roots remained concealed because such research has not concerned itself with the instinctual life of man. For instance Friedrich von der Leyden (1917) writes, "We now think that two well-known fairy tales—that of the werewold Allerleira and its human counterpart, the tale of Scaldhead, the exiled king's son who lives as a gardener's boy, conquers the other suitors by his extraordinary valor, and attains the hand of the King's daughter— lead back to the belief in werewolves." And about these sources, these strata of latent content of fairy tales, he adds

> Related to this paroxysm is a manifestation of illness or insanity that appeared among the old cultures in East and West and was reported, from examples in Germany and Russia, until deep into the seventeenth and eighteenth centuries, which still afflicts the Eastern population today and lives on as a saga in many places. That is the werewolf diseae, the illness where suddenly men are overcome with the conviction that they might be wolves or bears or also panthers or dogs, and behave like animals in a frenzy, roaming about at night, growling horribly, and attacking passers-by.

Psychoanalysis cannot consent to the attempt to trace the belief in werewolves only to anxiety about wild animals and to the usual tendencies of hermits and the mentally ill. It must refer to the sick it has studied, to the secret motivations in people often highly developed mentally and, not least, to experience with carefully observed and cooperative children. Sexual curiosity repeatedly plays the greatest role in the child's effort to bring something into its experience. There is a phase in the child's sexual conceptions in which the male sexual act is imagined as like the attack of the werewolf. This is an example of the way in which an instinctual source uncovers a deep link between child and fairy tale. The oedipus situation and its variants, the unloving mother, the stepmother the sibling relationship, provide the groundwork for the first psychoanalytic explanations of the motivation of fairy tale, such as Riklin and Rank have undertaken. Knowledge of the active instinctual demands in fairy tales is, however, more important for the pedagogue than is the consideration of whether this or that presentation is suitable, fitting, better or worse. In the first instance, the instincts active in the unconscious cannot be influenced directly by intellectual restrictions or considerations any more than movement in the interior of the earth is affected by what happens on its surface. On the contrary, we are frequently warned to pay attention to these movements and to build suitable houses in earthquake-prone regions.

As the grown man needs sleep—not only to prepare for the next day's work but to live a part of his inner life that he is unaware of, which his ordinary day does not allow him to live—so the child is ever again drawn back into a world in which the archaic, the outgrown, continues to live, because these elements are still alive in the child. If we were to ridicule and despise the fairy tale, as was done in the eighteenth century, this would indicate not supremacy over the child's instinctual demands but rather fear of them. If this anxiety is communicated to the child in any way, he must feel lonely and deserted in face of his instinctual wishes; he must stand in danger of being overcome by them; and this sense of being overwhelmed finds convincing expression in the nightmare.

It has been advocated that parents and educators should tell the fairy tales but should devalue them, treat them ironically, and present them as untrue. The effect of this approach is the denial of psychic facts, of impulses anchored in the unconscious (for example, the anxiety about devouring or being devoured), which make themselves known in the fairy tale. To the child, such denials of fact are equivalent to prohibitions. Yet one function of the fairy tale is to permit preoccupation with a part of the unconscious pressing for (magical) realization. There must be a basic misunderstanding here: fairy tales were first destined for adults, and the children listened to them. Only later did they become a means of education. As can happen with any such technique, the fairy tale was used in the service of cruel methods of education. It is customary to arouse in a child the fear of an instinctual impulse before its ego has actually been confronted with it. Thus a barrier is already set up which presses for repression of the instinct. I am thinking, for example, of the high tide of the Oedipus situation, or the onanistic phase linked to it. To the inner frustration (the result of the child's physical incapacity to gratify his instinctual demands, e.g., his incest wish), is added the external veto. Fairy tales serve these prohibitions: Sleeping Beauty, Hansel and Gretel, Red Ridinghood do not underline internally experienced frustrations and disappointments, they anticipate them. It is therefore a matter of some concern at what age of psychid development (which does not necessarily coincide with age phase) the child is told fairy tales. A certain development of the psychic personality, a differentiation, as we know from the structural theory of psychoanalysis (id-ego-superego), at any rate a time when the first ideal formations have been established, is one of the preconditions if a fairy tale is to fulfill its psychic function. The child must be near enough to the adult in his development so that he can become aware of a part of his unconscious without running any danger of being overwhelmed by his instincts.

Such a child can confront the stirring of his instinctual impulses with a touch of supremacy, he "plays with anxieties and dangers" which no longer exist. Just as the dream enforces a loosening of the boundaries between allowed and not-allowed, so the fairy tale reverses some of the inner and outer prohibitions to which the child is subjected from the beginning. The prohibitions and frustrations to which psychoanalysis refers are those that derive from the instincts, since everyone, irrespective of sex, race or class, must repress or modify some instinctual impulses for the benefit of other people. The child's most significant task is the adjustment to one of these instinctual impulses, the incest wish. This wish succumbs to repression, even in the most humane educational community in which any kind of outer frustration or threat of castration is omitted. The simple perception of a biological fact, the little girl's lack of a penis, suffices to achieve this result in boys. So long as abundant and unrestricted observations are not available to contradict this, we need not doubt that the child's incest wish is dealt with for internal reasons and that the educational milieu should only take care that meanwhile the child is subjected to the least possible disturbance from external influences. We know that during this internal process of repression the child is susceptible to great anxiety and that we should do everything possible not to exploit this anxiety readiness as a means of education. In this phase of development the child looks for threats of punishment because he experiences his incest wish as an offense against the other parent and seeks real satisfaction and atonement for this feeling of guilt. Here we can learn from the fairy tale because in it—and this is its charm and its greatest educational value—the story is so presented that the listener hears all the time the wishes and prohibitions that are common to us all. I think it is this mild dosage of prohibition, cruelty, and warrant that makes it impossible for the fairy tale to be a harmful influence in education. The pedagogue's question whether the lessening of prohibition by the fantasying in the fairy tale might not lead to a lifting of vetoes, may be answered in this way: the greater the denial of instinct that is required of a child, the greater the possibility of instinctual eruption. Pedagogues who use fairy tales only to underline prohibitions instead of making incest and other fantasies easier for the child, and who use such tales to threaten punishment, are more likely to meet with explosions in their pupils than are those who have grasped the child-conforming impulses in the fairy tale and have learned to tolerate that such impulses occur among children.

It may seem paradoxical that use of the fairy tale as an educational tool should be justified here from the standpoint of psychoanalytic thought, which one would expect to lay stress on the rational. The answer to this is that in modern educaiton a trend is becoming noticeable not only toward understanding instead of blind belief, but also toward a certain arrogance in rejecting the irrational in man, above all in the child. Here too, I fear, it is the thankless task of psychoanalysis to draw attention to things about which we would much rather not hear.

13

The Fight Against Masturbation in the Diary of an Adolescent

Masturbation can engage the attention of the educator either as a natural occurrence or as a problem in child rearing. His pedagogic attitude often prevents his being aware of this distinction. Usually educational action takes the place of scientific observation as a response to this natural manifestation. The view of the natural sciences should at least inform the pedagogue how seldom it is possible to influence not only the natural manifestation but the natural event itself. In the case of masturbation, education can at best suppress the immediate onanistic behavior but not the instinct pressing for gratification. In place of the suppressed masturbation, manifestations occur which we must call masturbatory equivalents. Recognition of these by pedagogues is very important because not only most "child misbehavior" but many harmless habits, too, are rooted in onanism and often make their first appearance or increase, after a prohibition of masturbation. They become a cause of perpetual dissatisfaction to adults or to the child himself. The ordinary educational apparatus—prohibition, good advice, diversion, providing a good example—is set in motion without success. It can result only in the appearance of another, new and possibly quite undetectable equivalent in place of the first, or in its temporary total disappearance, if the child can return to the original means of dealing with his instinct. From the fact of permitted masturbation equivalents and, above all, secret masturbation, one can see that education is not altogether so hostile to instinct and inhumane as the pedagogue's first reaction might often lead us to conclude: it contents itself with the visible, undesirable act being omitted and leaves to the child how much secret satisfaction he can provide for his instinctual demands. But the study of the neuroses has shown us that this being alone with one's instinct is not always advantageous to the child and that the outer contest between "misdeed" and education only reinforces the internal battle between wanting to and being able to, so that the result of a successful education may be neurotic illness. We know that this is both possible and probable if the instinctual life of the child comes into conflict with his conscience, his moral ideals, his superego, and that this can be the cause of subjective suffering in children as in adults.

It has repeatedly been argued that it is not the self-gratification but the *feeling of guilt* associated with it that produces the harmful effects of masturbation. This feeling of guilt plays a role in the life of the young that is not yet sufficiently appreciated; it is often a motive for socially significant activities. In so far as these issue from masturbation, they must be called acts of atonement. Whether writing a diary can be described as a socially valuable activity is an extra-psychological question of values, which Bernfield (1931) has dealt with, along with many other problems of diary keeping. In any case, guilt about masturbation is one motive for writing a diary, and on occasion it can become the sole means of discharging the pangs of conscience. That there is very seldom any mention of self-gratification in the diary in no way contradicts our assertion. The diary, in the main, does not serve at all as its writer intends, "to hold a mirror to oneself," "to see oneself," to unmask something, or whatever else is asserted. It is always more a description of the self with the intention of seeing it as one would like it to be. For example, one of the many motives for keeping a "chronicle" is to tell oneself that nothing else has happened except what is written down. We know that in this way the writer is confessing to just the opposite. Hence it would all depend on our finding the key to the code which would allow us to read the diary, as we read a carefully analyzed dream. Then we would find confirmation that the feeling of guilt about masturbation has its part in every one of these codes, that it is interwoven in everything else the youngster thinks and feels, and that his decisions are dependent on the outcome of this conflict with conscience, even when he allows others to decide for him. There can certainly be no question of our wishing to prevent this conflict, for the statement of psychoanalysis about its roots being grounded in development contradicts such a course. But it is not a matter of indifference to the youngster or to the society interested in him whether this conflict issues in health with or without defect. So long as it remains concealed from us, so long as pedagogues do not recognize it or know anything about it and, because they do not know what to do about it, do not want to know of it, one can have no hope of influencing the course and outcome of this developmental process.

I would like now to make a small contribution to this cipher key and make use of a youngster's diary as "code" for this purpose, because in it the cipher and its translation occur together. It is well known that such ciphers play a part in everyone's life and are understood by the unconscious of the one who uses them. Instances of parapraxis—slips of the tongue or of the hand, forgetting, and dream symbolism—are the everyday techniques of code makers, but deciphering is not always made so easy as it is by our youngster, K.J. I will cite here only the first page of his diary, leaving out a few lines that I will refer to later.

Tuesday, 16 March 1922, midday.
Cowardly timidity at last overcome. Now I want to begin to work. That Caesar goes round and round in my head. Who knows what will come of it? It will take a bit of work, meanwhile I will prepare very hard for the translation of the Gallic War and study Cicero, Sully and Sallust. Going on as I am now will get me nowhere. I can't upset the whole thing. Catalina or Ariovist, one of them must go by the board.

Wednesday, 7 June 1922.

Giving way to my own will ["will" crossed out] drive. This time for good. O that I could be strong. I must get to be. What I can do must become a match for what I wish; though can it? Much is passing through this breast. Should I let the imprisoned doves go free and hunt others? I must do so if I don't want to sink back into the dust of the rabble. [All that follows is crossed out]. The good will of the people is the best pledge. Let this be my motto. I want to believe!

Sunday, 16 June 1922.

I want to get out of this narrow and my soul thirsts for freedom. O Thou great God, have pity!

Wednesday, 12 August 1922.

Back home offensive, lazy, undecided, only old thoughts.

I must leave it to the reader whether he can already see from these lines what K.J. would be able to acknowledge only with contempt for himself and whether he, the reader, uses those passages in which the writer sketches his frame of mind or those which portray the conflict over the description of part of a Roman story. Everything that is expressed here about good intentions and about reflections about whether it would be better to do this or omit that, is a portrait of the fight against masturbation. The threats and self-loathing, the prayer for pity are the reaction to be worsted in this battle. This is confirmed by an entry on the first page of the diary, just after that of midday, Tuesday 16th May. The original version was as follows:

Evening

"Almost in despair, already again, now I undertake that I must never do it. Once more and I shall be finished for myself and for the world."

In writing about "despair" (*Verzweifeln*) K.J. had to correct himself. He first used a coined word *Verschweifeln* and indicated his mistake in an addendum so that this part of the diary now appeared as:

Catalina or Ariovist, one of them must go by the board.
Evening
Almost in despair (Verzweifeln), [inserted later: On 24 June, 1923,
I masturbated then] already again, now I undertake that I must
never do it. Once more and I shall be finished for myself and for
the world.]
Wednesday, 27 June 1922.
Giving way to my own will, drive etc.

It is well known that Freud's discoveries in his study of neuroses
have found confirmation in the study of primitive people, children,
and the insane; in the last named because above all they know and
tell in their hallucinations much more than would ever be possible
for "normal" people. We may ask ourselves why K.J. did not
conceal his masturbation as youngsters generally do. In the first
place he contented himself by indicating it behind the ciphers
usually encountered in many diaries; later his code (Verschweifeln)
became cleare; a year later he wrote openly about it. I can offer as an
explanation that two years later (in April 1924) he suffered a
temporary mental illness, after which he has now been capable of
following an occupation for five years.

It is because so many other youngsters with similar conflicts hide
them better—from themselves as well as from the surrounding
world—that I have chosen this example, in which the normal
mechanisms of concealment can be seen together with their
translation. If we bear in mind that the youngster's fight against
masturbation is the result of conflict between his instinctual life and
his moral sense and that this morality is concerned not only with
changeable, socially anchored morality but with that which is
strengthened by the adjustment to the incest wish, then no means
will appear to educators as too insignificant to pursue in attempting
to penetrate these tangled and hidden events in the adolescent. This
understanding cannot help but influence the way we meet,
understand, and regard young people, and, finally, the way they
view us.

14

The Psychoanalytic Approach to Education

Since psychoanalysis came into being, its data and theory have had an increasing influence on educational doctrine and theory. This is because it has always focused interest on individual history and especially on childhood development. Thus certain behavior disorders which in pre-analytic days were considered evidence of simulation or naughtiness are now considered manifestations of neurotic conflicts or fairly normal accompaniments of growth. It would be a mistake, however, to assume that the relation between psychoanalysis and education has developed beyond its infancty. Even the most optimistic can only say that during the years since its inception, psychoanalysis has had some remarkably successful applications to education.

Three facts have now been realized: first, that the teachings of psychoanalysis in regard to childhood and adolescence cannot in the future be confined to a chapter or two of general instruction but must become a subject for postgraduate study; second, that child analysts and educators must work together; and third, that though the main demand for psychoanlaytic instuction now comes from social workers, clinical psychologists, teachers and workers in special institutions (like the Southard School, Menninger Clinic, Topeka), the interest of all kinds of educators in its preventive possibilities will gradually be enlisted.

Some plans have already been considered. In its Five-Year Report (1932-37) The Chicago Institute for Psychoanalysis states:

During the past year the demand on the part of teachers and schools for psychoanalytic instruction and consultation has definitely increased. Although our children's department is now restricted to complementing our research work on adults, the Institute has been conscious since its foundation of the great importance of instructing educators and parents in the principles of personality development. This represents the future yield of preventive work. We are equally convinced of the importance of a large scale consultation service for educators and parents. Yet we feel as we did at the time of the publication of our last annual report, that this important task should not be undertaken in a haphazard way but requires careful organization. Although its social importance is beyond question, the Institute, in its present form, devoted as it is primarily to teaching and research in psychoanalysis, cannot undertake this complex task. Such an undertaking would require a number of additional analysts on our staff, child analysts, and specially trained social workers, indeed a separate division.

(A separate division of this type existed from 1932-38 in the Vienna Institute for Psychoanalysis; a short report of its experience was presented at the International Psycho-Analytical Congress in Paris, 1938).

Logical as these plans for collaboration may be from the point of view of the professional psychoanalyst, skepticism is aroused when one realizes how hard it is to put them into practice. During the past thirty years whole series of lectures have been arranged for educators but with a few exceptions, among which social workers have played an important part, they have not led to the desired results. On the one hand, the psychological interest of the educator must be profound to begin with, if he is to undertake an intensive study of psychoanalysis successfully, many educators need not only a "training analysis" but a personal character or therapeutic analysis. The most promising experiments with the most talented collaborators may still be frustrated by the limitations imposed on them by school authorities. On the other hand, psychoanalysts deterred by such adverse experiences often do not realize the immense changes that have occurred in the educational profession and the heightened qualification of the average modern educator. As a matter of fact, the history of "psychoanalytic education" does include two experiments with selected groups of educators, which were unfortunately terminated by external interference. One of these is credited to the Psychoanalytic Institute in Berlin at the peak of its activities after the First World War and the other to the Vienna Institute during the ten years before the 1938 Anschluss. Both experiments were possible only because the psychoanalysts conducting them had themselves been actively engaged in educational work for many years. They were well aware of the basic differences between a therapeutic-analytic approach and an educational-analytic approach to the child. It was clear to them that a catalyst was necessary.

This catalyst, child analysis, has brought about an ever closer and more fruitful exchange of functions between education and therapy. Now that psychoanalysis has been enriched in this way by the knowledge of forces and mechanisms at work in the child, what can it actually offer to education? Can it do more than remedy the failures, i.e., supplement customary methods in education? Can it make a direct contribution by teaching how failures may be reduced or even avoided? Or can psychoanalysis go beyond this reform work and offer new concepts, techniques, and aims to educators? These questions are not merely speculative, yet they can be answered only after educators and psychoanalysts have met and worked together experimentally for a considerable number of years, and, if possible, concerned themselves with all branches of education.

THE THERAPEUTIC APPLICATION

Charcot subjected children suffering from hysterical fits to exploration under hypnosis. Freud, however, stated in the earlier years of his work (1898) that his own method "demands a certain measure of clear-sightedness and maturity in the patient and is therefore not suited for youthful persons and for adults who are feeble-minded or uneducated." But he thought "it very probably that supplementary methods may be arrived at for treating young persons." The account of the first experimental treatment was published eleven years later in the well-known "Analysis of a Phobia in a Five-Year-Old Boy" (1909). The prerequisites for this analysis were Freud's doctrines of infantile sexuality (with the Oedipus complex) and of the unconscious, and the slightly modified technique of free association and interpretation; it was conducted only because of the father's active interest in psychoanalysis. But when one thinks of the specific difficulties encountered in subsequent attempts at child analysis one wonders whether it was really mere chance that the first analysis of a child's neurosis was carried out by a person so closely related to the patient. Implications for the function of parents and of the whole environment are involved here; and the problem has no little bearing on the relationship of psychoanalysis to education.

There were several other early attempts to bring psychoanalytic help to neurotic children. At the time "Little Hans" was published, A Swiss pastor, Oskar Pfister, started work along similar lines with young members of his religious community (1912). Activities like these appealed to many people, incluing teachers (e.g. Hans Zulliger), in spite of the generally strong opposition they met from psychologists, physicians, and educators. Pfister's approach to the child's neurosis and character abnormalities, though now considered obsolete, was certainly not ineffective (1922). A comparison with the analysis of Little Hans suggests again that the role of paternal, familial, or social authority cannot be neglected. In adult analysis the cure is carried forward by the patient's suffering, his will to recover and his transference; social resistances are thus overcome. In child analysis, however, one had to take into account, besides the child's immaturity, his ever-present fear of punishment, and his fear of disloyalty to parents, God, or the social code—powers which at that time no outsider dared challenge. The child's resistance was not of a psychological nature, as we understood it, but of a social nature; therefore the question of technique did not obtain until the social resistance had been overcome. This could only be achieved if the child's father or father-substitute, such as the head of the religious or school community, became clearly involved in the analytic activity.

The next major contributor, Hermine Hug-Hellmuth (1921), was eager to disentangle analytic and educational processes from each other. She intended to be the first psychoanalyst to establish child analysis as a special branch of education in cases where the child was unmanageable within his family and in urgent need of treatment. Her primary concern was to harmonize psychoanalytic aims with those of the family, school, and society. No doubt most of the children she had to deal with showed not only the usual signs of neurosis and unsuccessfully concealed anxiety but also a certin degree of social deterioration which, because of the psychological neglect by the family, overshadowed the basic psychoneurotic conflicts. Hug-Hellmuth's first step was to practice psychoanalysis in the child's home or in a children's ward. Thus she made herself to some extent independent of the parents' and the child's will to cooperate and confined child analysis to a mere buffer function in an environment interested not in her method but only in the final result of her work. From personal experience I can say that Hug-Hellmuth spent most of of her effort in finding out secrets that the child had intentionally withheld form educators—and thus she opened the door to the child's fantasy life. As she did so, the child tended more and more to act out his conflicts, to the great bewilderment of his family. This, of course, often endangered the continuation of the treament; however, where it did continue, improvement often followed and sublimation took place. In other words, these attempts were mainly characterized by the treatment of symptoms in children of latency and prepubertal age. They were aimed at better adaptation to the environment by alleviating superego demands and by encouraging the sublimation of instinctual drives. It was not desired that personality changes should be effected through the release of instinctual drives. This does not mean that repression was not occasionally resolved nor instinctual impulses tolerated. Sexual curiosity was certainly noted and satisfied through enlightenment, and parental prohibitoin of masturbation was lifted. But on the whole the tendency was to release only as much of the repressed instinctual tension and anxiety as could immediately be diverted into sublimation and not into conscious fantasies and acts. The concept of renunciation played little part, if any, because analysis did not proceed to the fixation point of the specific fantasies.

Thus psychoanalytic education at the end of the First World War meant almost exclusively the application of certain principles of analytic therapy. To become a psychoanalytic educator meant to become a therapist seeking to "cure neurotic children." The ensuing development was largely determined by two reactions to the advancing insight into Freud's work: one came from the group of educators who doubted whether therapy could serve as a preventive measure in a changed educational system; the other came from the group of professional psychoanalysts who insisted that all the conditions of pschoanalytic treatment be observed. It was not claimed that psychoanalytic therapy was the only means of dealing with behavior or personality disorders in the immature, but that its applicability to children had first of all to be evaluated under strictly therapeutic conditions; other practical considerations should be postponed until principles of child analysis had been established.

The outstanding names in modern child analysis, Anna Freud (1929) and Melanie Klein (1932), are now widely known. The bearing of their concepts upon education is naturally of interest. The educational implications of the Kleinian concept are almost entirely negative: "Deep psychology" is considered to be solely the realm of the professional psychoanalyst, and the antithesis of educational psychology. Accordingly, it follows that observations made by parents in the home are irrelevant for the task of the child analyst. Anna Freud's work, however, has opened new, positive, and promising channels for the development of educational doctrine.

What is the relationship of Anna Freud's technique to the child's education in home and school during its analysis? Briefly, it is determined by the degree of the child's immaturity. When the immaturity is great yet does not amount to contraindication, analyst and educator must cooperate extensively; with children less immature, as in advanced prepuberty or adolescence, the analysis will gradually resemble that of adults. The psychoanalytic procedure is not itself educational. Analysis is retrospective, concerned with the past, but of course it is not merely that. When it associates itself with the patient's ego, however immature, to alleviate superego demands, to correct fantasies about the parents or to release sexual and aggressive drives, the attitude of family and school may become of some importance. For instance, when fantasies become active, they result in instinctual eruptions such as indulgence in autoerotic activities, aggressiveness, hypochondriasis, eating and excretory disturbances and, most of all, anxiety states. In this respect child analysis will have periods of anti-educational effect and will put a greater strain on educators than would a full-blown, untreated disorder that had been controlled by purely educational measures.

During a child analysis, the emotional involvements of the environment also come into play. The mother's difficulties have been clearly described by Dorothy Burlingham (1935). Teachers, social workers and pediatricians may show similar reactions, not entirely attributable to irrational motives. I am not thinking here of unanalyzed educators, whose motives may be mere curiosity and professional envy, but of those who work with children most rationally and devotedly.

On the basis of her experience Anna Freud demands close cooperation between child analyst and educator. The inference is that child analysis can be carried out only in an analytic milieu, just as surgery, epidemiology, and pediatrics can be successful only under favorable conditions. This point of view should have a far-reaching influence on the organization of educaitonal facilities in which prevention of neuroses and early treatment are desired.

Now that child anlaysis has been freed of its earlier limitations it will certainly contribute more and more to our knowledge of psychological disorders. But it will probably not achieve broad social range for many years to come. To overcome this inherent handicap, its educational implications should be fostered and not rejected as troublesome, unworthy or fantastic.

Furthermore, child analysis is an invaluable instrument for psychoanalytic research, but its future is in no way secured; there are now only a few experienced child analysts and the temptation is strong among some to change over to full-time adult analysis. This is understandable but the danger for the future is that child anlaysis will be taught by analysts less experienced in it than is desirable. Even more serious is the likelihood that, if the manifestations of infantile neuroses are dealt with by strictly educational methods (naturally without effectively touching base conflicts), the need for adult analysis later will be greatly increased. Educators should be helped to understand these facts. A basis for collaboration with them must be provided. Until it has, we cannot tell what far-reaching effects child analysis may have on educational method and doctrine.

THE PREVENTIVE APPLICATION

The shadows caused by pathology lead scientists to look for the lights of prevention. Yet in psychological prevention, on which much thought and effort has been spent, one still feels rather in the dark. One envies the physiologist and pathologist who can give definite though limited advice about how to control such evils as dental caries, or the more common infectious diseases, postural abnormalities or flat feet. It is useless to blame social organization for the lack of psychological prevention so long as so little is known of its real nature. The experiences of the past thirty to forty years suggest that for a better understanding one should try to think in terms of generations rather than in terms of years and of large groups rather than of single cases. Psychoanalytic prevention, however, only aims at establishing the psychological bases of mental disorders and finding techniques to avoid them. It certainly cannot attempt to direct behavior in surroundings alien or hostile to psychological ways of thought. It must therefore be the domain of the educator. From the very beginning Freud himself encouraged us to think not only of cure but also of how to minimize or prevent the "traumatic effects of education on children." Presently we shall consider a series of suggestions that have emerged during the rapid development of psychoanalysis. A synthesis was suggested by Freud in his later papers, but so far it has not proceeded to its necessary experimental state because the precursors of prevention—child analysis and the training of educators—have themselves not yet passed the trial stage.

Here, as in medicine, the scope of prevention is conditioned by clinical experience and not by preconveived ideas as to what a human being should look like or how he should behave. It began with "the sexual traumas of childhood," the effect of the seduction of children by playmates or adults, which was thought to lead to "premature sexual excitation," and in turn to either hysterical or obsessional neurosis (Freud, 1896). But before clinical experience could begin to supersede the ancient moral attitude, the whole complex of infantile sexuality as a regular phenomenon in the evolution of human sexuality had to be described (Freud, 1905). This caused a complete change in the clincal concept of neuroses and perversions. It appeared that education clearly played a double part in the evolution of neuroses: on the one hand, by stimulation of infantile sexuality during the normal processes of growth, and on the other, by suppression of their most direct manifestations; the former possibly leading to the formation of fixations, the latter to repression and other mechanisms of shutting out instinctual demands from consciousness. The Scylla and Charybdis of all education, overindulgence and overfrustration, were established (Freud, 1933).

The basis of psychoanalytic education has now become far more complicated but for our present purpose of studying methods of preventive education, the following description may be sufficient. For a long period subsequent developments centered around the question of how to avoid pathogenic repression of instincts. Thus educators turned the course of preventive education toward the Scylla of giving way to the natural drives. Results were largely dependent upon the social and religous milieu from which the children came. Two groups of infantile sex drives had to be faced; the autoerotic pleasures, which are practically inaccessible to direct educational method, and those pleasures that demand an object.

Educators can affect only the latter. Thus it is hardly surprising that sexual curiosity became the first sphere for the application of preventive measures (Freud, 1907). It was known from adult analyses that early repression of sexual curiosity played an important part in the fixation of infantile sex theories, common to neurotics and perverts. But what does "satisfaction of sexual curiosity" in children mean? To some it meant giving the child complete information about the facts of adult sex life in order to end once and for all the child's craving for sexual knowledge. This may have been correct in cases where the child's manifest curiosity expressed a need for permission to know and to share in fantasy the relationship between the parents. But sexual curiosity sets in before the oedipal situation reaches its height and shows a pleasure-seeking character very early, like the normal curiostiy of adults. Moreover it is independent of direct educational interference. The child's own body and bodily functions (or those of other children and animals) can be used for gratification. These facts ought to have been taken into account by psychoanalytically influenced sex reformers, since Freud very early drew attention to infantile sex theories (1905). Erik Homburger Erikson (1930) and, more recently, Anna Freud (1944) have again tried to impress on educators the broader implications of sexual curiosity for intellectural development.

Just after the First World War emphasis shifted from the problem of sexual enlightenment to that of sex education. Attention was now to be directed to the pleasure-seeking sexual interests as a whole and not merely to sexual curiosity. The object was to minimize the frustration of instinctual demands, to avoid castration fear and the condemnation of sexual activities. The child's right to enjoy his instincts was to be actively encouraged. It was thought that the child needs to be hardened against unavoidable interference from persons who do not share his parents' views and that if natural development were to proceed unhampered, gradual progress would follow automatically according to the stages described by Freud. Thumb-sucking, pleasure in dirt, smearing, exhibitionism and scoptophilia, masutrbation and attempts at intercourse were expected to give way step by step to the normal processes of the latency period. Such experiments, spread over a number of years, could only be carried out of parents who themselves had a fair knowledge of the development of the instincts. When the child reached school age his sex education, free from the usual traumatic interference, would be complete; he would settle down to normal activities, less hampered by repression and more inclined to sublimation. Furthermore, it was hoped that with the relaxing of conventional education, neuroses would be prevented. Children brought up in this way were also expected to feel safer when exposed to sexual experiences at school or in the street.

Much stress was naturally laid on the management of the oedipal situation. Masturbation was not restricted; expressions of jealousy were encouraged; the parents' bodies were not hidden from the child's sight; curiosity, which we now believe was excitement, was satisfied, and information willingly given; expressions of hate and discontent were never disapproved. Special care was taken when a younger child was about to be born; the changes in the mother's body were no secret; the child was permitted to take part in the preparations for the newcomer, and his reactions after the birth were carefully watched. In general, there was a tendency to aovid any form of prohibition. The mother did not threaten to withdraw her love when her own and the child's wishes were antagonistic. Parental authority was replaced by the explanation of all demands and the constant appeal to the child's insight and affection. Authoritative demands were condemned because they were considered sadistic and likely to cause castration fear.

Some experiments with psychoanalytic group education were based on similar concepts. Vera Schmidt (1925) ran a home in Moscow for children under five entirely according to these principles and reported very favorable results in sexual and personality development. She also stressed the untoward effect of this form of education on the emotional life of nurses and nursery teachers who had not been analyzed. Most of them broke down after a few months. Similar results were reported by Bernfeld (1922) on a home for war orphans (Baumgarten) opened shortly after the First World War. Both experiments were short-lived and do not allow definite conclusions to be drawn about group education. Aichhorn's experiences (1923) with socially and psychologically neglected adolescents were more favorable. His individual work with juvenile delinquents was even then based on concepts different from those of the postwar period (1918-1924). Some of the experiences Hans Zulliger reported (1941) were based on similar ideas.

To the surprise of those who had advocated it, psychoanalytically-based sex education did not yield satisfactory results; many cases of character disturbance and behavior disorder became known among children brought up on these lines. It is true that in comparison with children reared in the conventional way, these children seemed less inhibited (i.e., they had less respect for the needs of adults). They were brighter and showed a variety of interests and talents, but they were often less curious about the world of objects. They had no perseverance and easily relapsed into daydreaming, which made them appear introverted. They clung to many infantile habits, which gave them cheap consolation in the face of disappointments. Periodically some showed lack of control of bodily functions, e.g., enuresis or encopresis. They very readily gave vent to emotions that vanished as quickly as they appeared. Thus the changes expected during the latency period did not occur; only a limited reduction of instinctual expression could be observed. Normal school life put a great strain on children and teachers. Even in modern schools these children showed comparatively little spontaneity and their concentration was disturbed. They seemed egocentric; group demands affected them little. They were extremely intolerant of the demands of adults; timetables, mealtimes, table manners, routine hygienic measures, even if leniently handled, became sources of conflict. Traffic policemen and park keepers were regarded as main public enemies. The children were involved in a constant struggle against a world full of demands and duties. It became clear that their education did not harmonize with the restraints of city life.

To the psychoanalytically trained observer these children showed an unexpected degree of irritability, a tendency to obsessions and depressions, and certain peculiarities which during subsequent analytic treatment proved to be concealed anxiety. When these children reached the period of latency, development could not be revoked; psychoanalysis had to be called in to deal with the threatened deterioration of character.

How could the drawbacks of psychoanalytic education be explained? They had been caused not by an erroneous but by an incomplete application of analytic principles. The results of adult analysis had been applied too ridigly to sex education. After the First World War psychoanalysis progressed from a psychology of instincts to one of personality but it was still too early to make use of the newer concepts of ego and superego development. The paramount importance of the lack of early sex education in the elaboration of neurotic conflict had indeed been demonstrated; but the alternative to the old-fashioned neglect or denial of infantile sexuality is not to admit its existence and then leave the child alone with his various drives. This is merely another way of neglecting the immature organism. Besides the child's power and desire to enjoy pleasure from his own body there is the desire to be like an adult. This desire is anchored in the depth of the oedipal wishes, which are prone to frustration even without any external influence. To excite castration fear in the boy and penis-envy in the girl no other stimulation from the outside is necessary than the unavoidable sight of the other sex's genitals. Psychoanalytic education now must do more than protect the child's right to elaborate on his instincts. The child's poorly developed ego faces powerful instinctual sensations and tensions, which we call "internal dangers." In the human race instincts are controlled first by the ego and then by the superego. These considerations made necessary the next steps in the application of psychoanalysis to education.

THE EDUCATIONAL APPLICATION

Modern concepts in psychoanalytic education are based on a knowledge of the qualities the immature ego displays during the first five years of life. General experience suggests that the child's ego is weak, that the instincts constantly demand gratification from it, and that it needs care and support from the outside. It grows in strength and expands its activities in proportion to its ability to control component instincts and object-relationships. For this a strong narcissistic cathexis of the ego is necessary. Experience in psychopathology shows how the instinctual demands from inside and stimulation from outside (frustration) interfere with ego development—how, for instance, exaggerated maternal care may inhibit it by replacing ego functions. It is a commonplace that most children up to five, and certainly all those who later struggle with life neurotically, pass through periods of upheaval in which subsequent disturbances are rooted. Thus clinical considerations play an important part in psychoanalytic education in the same way that somatic pathology does in the physical care of young children. This fact distinguishes our line of thought from that of other schools in educational psychology (Hollingworth, 1934).

In the understanding of the "minor" neurotic disturbances of childhood emphasis has shifted from the role of the instincts to the role of the immature ego. Whereas during the period of purely preventive application, education was thought to act directly on the instincts—in consequence of which anxiety was aroused and the ego impoverished and restricted in its activity—today we believe that education acts on the ego itself, making use of its constant efforts to harmonize instincts and functions. This is demonstrated, for instance, in the young child's continual attempt to strike a balance between autoerotic drives and drives directed toward the mother-object. Left to himself the child of about fourteen months, as described by Freud long ago, regularly shows a liking for his bowel products. Playing with feces and enjoying their smell is a necessary stage in instinctual development. But in our culture it is opposed to the child's need to feel safe and in full possession of his mother or nurse. She does not actively share in these pleasures. The child's ego has to face two instinctual demands, and the mother's attitude definitely helps him to come to a decision. In these days the struggle usually ends in a compromise, the mother offering the child some substitute material to play with and smear. But if the anal component instinct is constitutionally strong and the child feels compelled to succumb to it, adaptation is more difficult; the ego may easily show reactions of anxiety and may need educational help, which, as psychopathology shows, often miscarries.

Any failure of this integrating and harmonizing function may result in a split of the immature ego, part of which may remain at a primitive level for many years or even for a lifetime. A tendency to anxiety may follow. The eventual outcome of this split will be decided by the constitutional disposition, the strength of other component instincts, the oedipal situation, and new identifications.

Clinical experience suggests that besides the tendency to anxiety, the sequel to the split in the ego is the formation of a specific primitve fantasy that solves the original conflict in a pleasurable way. Meanwhile, in its general development, the rest of the ego tends to follow the reality principle. Modern preschool education does much toward strengthening that part of the ego that tends toward reality, and thus supports, though often in vain, its efforts to keep instinctual demands outside of its organization. From the psychopathological point of view, anxiety is therefore a helpful sign that the integrating function of the ego has failed.

The oedipal situation and the subsequent formation of the superego puts the highest strain on the ego's ability to synthesize. The most pleasurable and therefore the least tractable of all the instincts, the genital instinct, and the strongest object-relationships have to be dealt with. Apart from the reports of the Hampstead Nurseries (A. Freud, 1944) little is known about the child's normal handling of this strenuous and most complicated period. The child of today seems little prepared to express emotions and fantasies verbally, and one may wonder whether the modern educator does not rely too confidently on play as abreaction. By the time the child enters the latency period his personality has assumed definite form. Superego demands will deepen the gulf between the integrated personality and the unconscious fantasies, which will take advantage of any weakening of the ego in sleep, illness, or any other contingency. Emotional disturbances, anxiety states, and neurotic symptoms may now become obvious and of social importance.

The problem of antisocial behavior and delinquency deserves special consideration. The manifestations of faulty integration naturally change with growth and with a changing environment. Hence antisocial behavior that has not developed in an antisocial environment almost always has a neurotic background dating from early childhood. In such children, too, it appears that a specific fantasy is the fundamental psychological structure which stimulates the delinquent trends during latency. Aichhorn (1923) holds the view that some types of delinquents who have not been socially neglected, notably the impostor type, need treatment in two stages, spread over a number of years; the first stage aims at transforming the antisocial character traits into neurotic symptoms: the second deals with the neurotic-perverted personality, which in its emotional regression approximates to patterns of early childhood. This is not to imply that the first stage should not bring about socially desirable changes.

The educator cannot reach the child's basic neurotic conflicts during latency or puberty. The appropriate treatment of all conditions that involve the superego is child analysis. Other methods, though they may be of high social importance, can only rarely reach etiological levels. All further progress, however, will be dependent on the further increase of scientific data.

There is a "crying need for the results of longitudinal research on personality development" (Sears, 1944). No amount of successful child analyses and no miracles that well-trained educators and parents may report can replace a prolonged experiment with children and adolescents from birth to maturity. Only after the experience of such research shall we be able to assess whether or not it is possible to prevent or modify early traumas and to what extent the ego's ability to integrate id tendencies can be developed and utilized.

List of Publications

(Chapter nos. given to papers included in this volume.)

1922   Ein Knabenbund in einer Schulgemeinde. In *Vom Gemeinschaftsleben der Jugend; Beitraege zur Jugend-Forschung,* ed. S. Bernfeld. Leipzig: Int. Psa. Verlag. (Trans. Chap. 8)

1924   Phantasiespiele der Kinder und ihre Beziehung zur dichterischen Produktiontat. In *Vom dichterischen Schaffen der Jugend: neue Beitraege zur Jugendforschung.* ed. S. Bernfeld. Leipzig: Int. Psa. Verlag. (Trans. Chap. 10)

1926   Ueber die Maennliche Latenz unde ihre Spezifische Erkrankung. *Zeitschrift 12.*

1931   Der Onaniekampf im Tagebuch des Jugendlichen. Psa. Pa. 5. (Trans. Chap. 13)

1931   Kind und Maerchen, *Psa. Pa. 5.* (Trans. Chap. 12)

1932   Der Arzt in der Beziehungsberaten, *Psa. Pa. 6.*

1932   Das Archaische im Spiel. Psa. Pa. 6. (Trans. Chap. 11)

1936   Bericht ueber die Einleitung einer Kinderanalyse.

1940   Analyse einer postenche palitischen Geistesstoerung. *Int. Zeit. Psychoanal. 25.*

1945   Psychoanalytic education. *Psychoanalytic Study of the Child* 1. (Chap. 14)

1946   Diaries of adolescent schizophrenics. *Psychoanalytic Study of the Child* 2.

1949   Mouth, hand and ego integration. *Psychoanalytic Study of the Child* 3/4. (Chap. 1) Trans. *Psyche* 18.

1950a   Oral aggressiveness and ego development. *Int. J. Psycho-Anal.* 31. (Chap. 2)

1950b   Development of the body ego. *Psychoanalytic Study of the Child* 5. (Chap. 3)

1950c   Three psychological criteria for the termination of treatment. *Int. J. Psycho-Anal.* 31.

1952   Mutual influences in the development of ego and id; earliest stages. *Psychoanalytic Study of the Child* 7. (Chap. 4)

1954a   Defensive process and defensive organisation, *Int. J. Psycho-Anal.* 35.

1954   North American psychiatry. Letter to *Lancet*, 11 December, 1954.

1955   *Some current problems of psychoanalytic training and research.* Twelfth Series Abraham Flexner Lectures, published for Vanderbilt University by the Williams & Wilkins C., Baltimore. Lecture 6, "Some problems of ego psychology," forms Chap 5. Lecture 4, "Some aspects of the psychoanalytic investigation of childhood," forms Chap. 6.

1955   Transference and transference neurosis. *Int. J. Psycho-Anal.* 37.

1956   Medicine since Freud. Contribution to the *Observer*. Freud centenary series, "The Meaning of Freud."

1959   Der getaeuschte Hochstapler. Contribution to Aichhorn Festschrift *Aus der Werkstatt des Erziehungs Beraters*. Vienna: Verlag fur Jugend und Volk. Trans. "The Deceiver Deceived," *Searchlights on Delinquency*.

1962   Eine Therapeutische Illusion. *Jahrbuch der Psychoanal.* 2. (translation of 1961 pre-Congress address, not published in English)

1964   Die Revolution geht vielleicht weiter. Contribution to series "Was ist von Freud geblieben?" *Forum* (Vienna) 11.

1965   Review of *Minutes of the Vienna Psychoanalytic Society* Vol. I. 1906-1908. Ed. H. Nunberg & E. Federn. New York: Int. Univ. Press, 1962, *Int. J. Psycho-Anal.* 46. German trans. *Psyche* 19.

1965   Siegried Bernfeld and Jerubbaal. *Leo Baeck Institute Yearbook* 10. (Chap. 9)

1967   Bermerkungen zur Abwehrlehre. Contribution to *Hoofdstukken uit de Hedensdaagse Psychoanalyse*. Ed. P.J. van der Leeuw, E.C. Frijling and P.C. Kuiper in honor of Jeanne Lampl-de-Groot's 70th birthday. Arnhern: Von loghum Slaterus.

1967   Contribution to discussion on A.J. Lubin's "The Influence of the Russian Orthodox Church on Freud's Wolf-Man: A hypothesis," *Forum* (Los Angeles) 2.

"Infant Observations and Concepts Relating to Infancy," the Freud Anniversary Lecture delivered in New York in spring of 1966, is printed by permission of the New York Psychoanalytic Association. It forms Chap. 7.

Bibliography

Abraham, K. (1909). Trauma und Mythos. *S.Z.A.S.* 5. Translated in *Selected Papers*. London: Hogarth, 1927.

Aichhorn. A. (1923). Ueber die Erziehung in Bessergungs-Anstalten, *Imago* 9.

_____ (1935). *Wayward Youth*. New York: Viking.

Balint, A. (1939). Love for the mother and mother-love. *Int. Z. Fuer Psa.* 24; (1949) *Int. J. Psycho-Anal.* 30.

Balint, M. (1937). Early developmental states of the ego: Primary object-love. *Imago* 24; (1949) *Int. J. Psycho-Anal.* 30.

_____ (1945). Individual differences of behaviour in early infancy and an objective method for recording them. M.Sc. thesis, Manchester University.

Bernfeld, S. (1913). Das Archiv fuer Jugendkultur. *Der Anfang* 1.

_____ (1916). Die Kriegswaisen. *Der Jude* 1.

_____ (1919). *Das Juedische Volk und seine Jugend*. Vienna: Loewi Verlag.

_____ (1921). *Kinderheim Baumgarten: Bericht uber einer ernsthaften Versuch mit neuer Erziehung*. Berlin: Juedische Verlag.

_____ (1922). *Vom Gemeinschaftsleben der Jugend: Beitraege zur Jugendforschung*. Leipzig: Int. Psychoanal. Verlag.

_____ (1925). *Psychologie des Saeuglings*. Vienna: Julius Springer Verlag.

_____ (1929). *The Psychology of the Infant*. New York: Brentano.

_____ (1931). *Trieb und Tradition im Jugendalter*. Leipzig: Int. Psycho-Anal. Verlag.

Bing, J., F. McLaughlin and R. Marburg (1959). The metapsychology of narcissim. *Psychoanalytic Study of the Child*.

Bowlby, J. (1944). Forty-four juvenile thieves: their characters and home life. *Int. J. Psycho-Anal.* 25.

_____ (1951). *Maternal Care and Mental Health*. Geneva: World Health Organization.

Brierley, M. (1951). *Trends in Psycho-Analysis* London: Hogarth.

Brody, S. (1956). *Patterns of Mothering*. New York: Int. Univ. Press.

Buber, Martin (1963). Zion und die Jugend. In *Der Jude und sein Judentum*. Meltzer: Koeln.

Buhler, K. (1921). *Die Geistige Entwicklung der Kinder.* Jena.

Burlingham, D.T. (1935). Child analysis and the mother. *Psychoanal. Quart.* 4.

_____ and A. Freud (1943). *War and Children.* New York: Int. Univ. Press; London: Allen & Unwin.

_____ and A. Freud (1944). *Infants without Families.* New York: Int. Univ. Press.

Carr (1902). *The Survival of Play Values.* Colorado.

Deutsch, H. (1922). Ueber die pathologische Luege. *Zeitschrift fuer Psycho-Anal.* 8.

Erikson, E.H. (1935). Psychoanalysis and the future of education. *Psychoanal. Quart.* 4.

Escalona, S. (1950). See Leitch and Escalona.

Federn, P. (1924). Maerchen, Mythos, Urgeschichte. In Federn-Meng *Volksbuch.* Stuttgart.

Fenichel, O. (1942). Symposium on neurotic disturbances in Sleep. *Int. J. Psycho-Anal.* 23.

Ferenczi, S. (1916). Stages in the development of the sense of reality. In *Contributions to Psychoanalysis.* Boston: R.G. Badger, 1926.

Fisher, C. (1965). Psychoanalytic implications of recent research on sleep and dreaming. *J. Amer. Psychoanal. Assoc.* 13.

Five Year Report (1932-37). Chicago Institute for Psychoanalysis.

Freud, A. (1922). Schlagphantasie und Tagtraum. *Imago* 1.

_____ (1929). *Introduction to the Technique of Child Analysis.* Nervous & Mental Disease Monograph 48.

_____ (1937). *The Ego and the Mechanisms of Defence.* London: Hogarth; New York: Int. Univ. Press, 1940.

_____ (1943). See Burlingham und Freud.

_____ (1944). See Burlingham and Freud.

_____ (1944). Sex in childhood. *Health Education J.* 2.

_____ (1946). The psychoanalytic study of infantile feeding disturbances. *Psychoanalytic Study of the Child* 2.

_____ (1947). The establishment of feeding habits. In Ellis, R.B., *Child Health and Development.* Churchill.

_____ (1951). An experiment in group upbringing. *Psychoanalytic Study of the Child* 7.

_____ (1952a). The mutual influence in the development of the ego and the id. Introduction to discussion. *Psychoanalytic Study of the Child* 7.

_____ (1952b). Observations on child development. *Psychoanalytic Study of the Child* 7.

_____ (1952c). The role of bodily illness in the mental life of children. *Psychoanalytic Study of the Child* 7.

_____ (1953). Film review of "A two-year old goes to hospital" *Int. J. Psycho-Anal.* 34.

Freud, S. All references to Standard Edition (London, Hogarth) are abbreviated SE

_____ (1896). Further remarks on the defence-neuropsychoses. SE 3.

_____ (1898). Sexuality in the etiology of the neuroses. SE 3.

_____ (1905). *Three Essays on the Theory of Sexuality*. SE 7.

_____ (1907). The sexual enlightenment of children. SE 9.

_____ (1909). Analysis of a phobia in a five-year-old boy. SE 10.

_____ (1909). On the sexual theories of children. SE 9.

_____ (1911). Formulations on the two principles of mental functioning. SE 12.

_____ (1913). *Totem and Taboo*. SE 13.

_____ (1914). On narcissism. SE 14.

_____ (1915). Instincts and their vicissitudes. SE 14.

_____ (1917). A metapsychological supplement to the theory of dreams. SE 14.

_____ (1919). The uncanny. SE 17.

_____ (1923). *The Ego and the Id*. SE19.

_____ (1925). Negation. SE 19.

_____ (1926). *Inhibitions, Symptoms and Anxiety*. SE 20.

_____ (1933). *New introductory lectures*. SE 22.

Fries, M.E. and P.T. Woolf (1953). Some hypotheses on the role of the congenital activity type in personality development. *Psychoanalytic Study of the Child* 8.

Gesell, A. and F.L. Ilg (1937). *Feeding Behavior of Infants*. Philadephia: Lippincott.

_____ (1942). *Infant and Child in the Culture of Today*. New York: Harper.

Glover, E. (1939). *Psycho-Analysis*. London & New York: Staples.

_____ (1947). Basic mental concepts. Their clinical and theoretical value. *Psychoanal. Quart.* 16.

_____ (1950). Functional aspects of the mental apparatus. *Int. J. Psycho-Anal.* 31.

Gorer, G. and Rickman, J. (1945). The biological economy of birth. *Psychoanalytic Study of the Child*. 1.

Greenacre, P. (1952). *Trauma, Growth and Personality*. New York: Norton.

Grinstein, A. *The Index of Psychoanalytic Writings*. Bernfeld.

Gross, K. (1910). Das Spiel als Katharsis. *Zeitschrift fuer Paed. Psych.* 9.

Gross, W. (1959). The Zionist students' movement. *Yearbook of the Leo Baeck Institute* 4; London.

Hall, G.S. (1924). *Adolescence, its Psychology and its Relation to Physiology.* New York: Appleton & Co. 2 vols.

Hartmann, H. (1952). The mutual influences in the development of the ego and the id. *Psychoanalytic Study of the Child* 7.

———with Kris and R. Loewenstein (1946). Comments on the formation of psychic structure. *Psychoanalytic Study of the Child* 2.

Heath, R.G., ed. (1964). *The Role of Pleasure in Behavior.* New Orleans.

Hoffer, W. See List of Publications.

Hollingworth, L. (1934). Education. In *The Problem of Mental Disorder.* National Research Council, Committee on Psychiatric Investigation.

Hug-Hellmuth, H. (1921). On the Technique of Child Analysis. *Int. J. Psycho-Anal.* 2.

Ilg, F. (1937). See Gesell.

Isakower, O. (1938). A contribution to the pathopsychology of phenomena associated with falling asleep. *Int. J. Psycho-Anal.* 19.

Jacobson, E. (1954). The self and the object world. *Psychoanalytic Study of the Child* 9.

———(1965). *The Self and the Object World.* London: Hogarth.

Klein, M. (1932). *The Psycho-Analysis of Children.* London: Hogarth.

———(1942). The Oedipus complex in the light of early anxieties. *Int. J. Psycho-Anal.* 26.

———(1948). *Contributions to Psycho-Analysis* (1921-1945).

Kohn, E. (1922). The initiation rites of the historical professions. In Bernfeld's *Beitraege zur Jegendforschung.* Vienna: Int. Psa. Verlag.

Kris, E. (1946). See Hartmann, Kris and Loewenstein.

——— (1951). Opening remarks on psychoanalytic child psychology. *Psychoanalytic Study of the Child* 6.

Lampl-de Groot, J. (1947). On the development of the ego and super-ego. *Int. J. Psycho-Anal.* 28.

Leitch, M. and S. Escalona (1950). The reactions of infants to stress; report on clinical findings. *The Psychoanalytic Study of the Child* 3/4.

Leyden, F. von der (1917). *Das Maerchen, ein Versuch.* Quelle & Meyer.

Lewin, B.D. (1946). Sleep, the mouth and the dream screen. *Psychoanal. Quart.* 15.

———(1950). *Psychoanalysis of Elation.* New York: Norton; London: Hogarth.

Loewenstein, R. (1946). See Hartmann, Kris and Loewenstein.

Marburg, R. (1959). See Bing.

McLaughlin, F. (1959). See Bing.

Michaelis, D. (1962). Mein "Blau-Weiss Erlebnis. *Bulletin des Leo Baeck Insitut.* Tel Aviv: Verga Bitaon.

Middlemore, M.P. (1941). *The Nursing Couple.* London: Hamish Hamilton.

Monroe, (1899). Ueber die Entwicklung des sozialen Bewussteins. Berlin.

Nunberg, H. (1932). *Allgemeine Neurosenlehre.* Bern: Huber.

Pfeifer, S. (1919). Aeusserungen infantile-erotische Triebe im Spiel. *Imago.*

Pfister, O. (1922). *Psychoanalysis in the Service of Education.* London.

————— (1912). Anwendung der Psychoanalyse in der Pedagogik und Seelensorge. *Imago* 1.

Premier Congres Mondiale de Psychiatrie (1950) Paris. Herman et Cie.

Preyer, W. (1882). *Die Seele des Kindes.* Leipzig: Th. Grieben Verlag.

————— (1895). *The Mind of the Child.* New York: Appleton.

Rank, O. (1907). *Der Kuenstler.* Vienna: Heller.

————— (1912). *Das Inzestmotiv in Dichtung und Saga.* Leipzig, Vienna: E. Deuticke.

————— (1919). *Psychoanalytische Beitraege zur Mythenforschung.* Vienna.

Reik, W. (1928). *Das Ritual.* (Int. Psa. Verlag, Imago Buch 9).

Rickman, J., ed. (1936). *On the Bringing-Up of Children* by Five Psycho-Analysts. London: Kegan Paul.

————— (1945). See Gorer.

Riklin, F. (1908). *Wunscherfuellung und Symbolik im Maerchen.* 2 vols. Leipzig, Vienna: Deuticke. Trans. W.H. White. (1915). *Wishfulfillment and Symbolism in Fairy Tales.* Nervous & Mental Disease Monograph 21.

Report of Proceedings: Paris Congress 1939. *Int. J. Psycho-Anal.* 20.

Riviere, J. (1936). On the genesis of psychical conflict in earliest infancy. *Int. J. Psycho-Anal.* 17.

Robertson, J. (1952). A two-year-old goes to hospital: A scientific film record. London: Tavistock.

Rogers, C.H. (1939). *Play Therapy in Childhood.* Oxford Univ. Press.

Roheim, G. (1932). Psychoanalyse primitiver Kulturen. *Imago* 3/4.

Rubins, J.L. and E.D. Friedman (1948). Asymbolia for pain. *Archiv. Neuro-Psychiatry* 60.

Schmidt. V. (1925). *Psychoanalytische Erziehung in Sowjetrussland: Bericht ueber die Kinderheim Laboratorium in Moskau.*

Scott, W.C.E. (1946). A note on the psychopathology of convulsive phenomena in manic-depressive states. *Int. J. Psycho-Anal.* 27.

Searl, M.N. (1944). Some contrasted aspects of psychoanalysis and education. *Brit. J. Educational Psychology.*

Sears, E. (1944). *Survey of Objective Studies of Psychoanlaytical Concepts.* Social Science Research Council Report.

Shafer, E. (1965). Report on contributions of Longitudinal Studies to Psychoanalytical Theory.

Spence, J.C. (1947). Care of children in hospital. *Brit. Med. J.* 1.

Spitz, R.A. (1945). Hospitalism: an enquiry into the genesis of psychiatric conditions in early childhood. *Psychoanalytic Study of the Child* 1.

—— (1946). Anaclitic depression. *Psychoanalytic Study of the Child* 2.

—— (1965). *The First Year of Life.* New York: Int. Univ. Press.

Sully, J. (1896). *Studies in Childhood.* London.

Symposium on Child Analysis (1927). *Int. J. Psycho-Anal.* 8.

Tramer, H. (1962). Juedischer Wanderbund Blau-Weiss. Ein Beitrag seiner Aeusseren Geschichte. *Bullein des Leo Baeck Institut* 5. Tel Aviv: Verlag Bitaon.

Uexkull, J. von (1926). *Theoretical Biology.* London: Routledge & Kegan Paul.

Wiesenthal, G. (1919). *Der Aufstieg.* Berlin.

Winnicott, D.W. (1945). Primitve emotional development. *Int: J. Psycho-Anal.* 26.

—— (1951). The ordinary devoted mother and her baby. *Int. J. Psycho-Anal.* 30.

—— (1953). Transitional objects and transitional phenomena. *Int. J. Psycho-Anal.* 32.

Woolf, P.T See Fries.

Wyneken G. (1913). *Schule und Jugenkultur.* Jena: Eugen Dieterich.

Zulliger, H. (1941). Psychoanalytic experience in public school practice. *American J. of Orthopsychiatry* 11.

Index

delusions, structure of, 3
demanding reaction in ill child,
    71–72
dental interventions, psychological
    effect of, on child, 68, 70
depression, anaclitic, in infants,
    62–65
Deutsch, H., 162, 163
Dizendruck, Zur, 134
dream
  in infancy, 83–84
  of operation as initiation rite,
    170–72
dream screen, 3, 4, 80

education, psychoanalytic ap-
    proach to, 191–206
  educational application, 203–206
  preventive application, 198–203
  therapeutic application, 194–98
ego and id, mutual influences in de-
    velopment of, 29–41
  body as object of id drives, 31
  conclusion, 39–41
  internal milieu, 31–34
  and oral primacy and object,
    36–37
  problem of hallucination in early
    infancy, 34–36
  self and object, 38–39
  sleep and wakefulness, 37–38
ego development
  earliest phases of, 43–58
  and oral aggressiveness, 11–20
    concept of, 16–18
    and libidinization of body,
      19–20
    limitations of, 18
    observation, 12–16
    and pain barrier, 18–19

ego functions, Freudian, in infants,
    49
ego integration, mouth, hand and,
    3–10
Einstein, Albert, 144
Ekstein, R., xiv
environment, children's relation to,
    and developing self, 46–49
Erikson, E.H., 87, 200
Escalona, S., 46

fairy tales and child, 177–83
  non-psychoanalytic investigators
    of, 177–78
  psychoanalytic view of, 178–83
fantasy play, children's and poetic
    creativity, 145–64
  elaboration and changes in
    youthful shared, 148–56
  introduction, 146–48
  psychological meaning of, in la-
    tency, 156–60
  and relation of, to reality and re-
    pression, 160–63
  versus daydream and artistic
    creation, 163–64
Federn, P., 18, 37, 178
Fenichel, O., 3
Ferenczi, S., 14, 36, 78, 86, 152
fever, hypnagogic phenomena in, 3
Fisher, C., 83, 84, 85
Frankl, L., 88
Freud, A., ix-x, xii, 5, 12, 36, 40, 45,
    53, 57–58, 61, 62, 63, 66, 67,
    68, 72, 75, 79, 157, 196, 197,
    200, 205
Freud, S., xv, 4, 18, 19, 21, 22, 30,
    31, 32, 33, 34–35, 39, 40, 43,
    45, 49, 50, 60–61, 70, 75, 76,
    77, 78, 80, 82, 83, 84, 85, 86,